# A MOM'S GUIDE TO SCHOOL FUNDRAISING

## by Sarah Barrett

ISBN-13: 978-1481173216
ISBN-10: 1481173219

## <u>DEDICATION</u>

This book is dedicated to all the hard working moms and dads out there who do everything they can to help their kids have a well-rounded education. It's also dedicated to the amazing teachers who have helped me and who continue to help our children feel inspired, engaged and excited about learning! A big thank you to the parents all over the country who shared their fundraising successes with me for this book. Finally, a HUGE thank you to my husband, Andrew and my daughters. You have all taught me so much about life, love and the importance of giving back. Thank you for being patient and supportive of me – always!

4

# TABLE OF CONTENTS

Setting the Table:  Things you will want to know before you get started.
Making the Invitations:  How to get people and businesses involved.
> Seven Steps in setting up an effective Get Squad
> Sample Pitches
> Sample Phone Scripts
> Behavioral Email Marketing Messages for Parents
> Ten Basic Rules of Fundraising

*aka The Big Meals*
Annual Gift Donations
Partners in Education or Community Sponsorship
The Party Book
Auctions
> Live Auctions
> Online Auctions
> Silent Auctions

*aka Meals Where Kids Help With Preparation*
Walk-a-thon
Carnival
Book Fairs & Book Exchanges
Personalized Note Cards and more
Class Art Projects
Free Dress Days

# FOREWORD

When I was in elementary school, life was much simpler. To raise money for the booster club, our parents had bake sales and pancake breakfasts and even put on a parent talent show. The proceeds funded special assemblies and class trips. As part of our core curriculum, we had music, art, and library time and the entire 6th grade staged a full-length musical every year. We always had time to go out and play outside and learn basic games from our gym teacher, Mr. Harada.

Today, elementary school is very different...at least it is in California. If kids are lucky, they might get PE once or twice a week, but nothing like the program we had as kids. There's no money or time for drama or art. School libraries all over southern California are being closed because there's not enough funding to keep them open. Some schools don't even have enough toilet paper or soap for the children each day! What is a parent to do?

When I was a kid, moms and dads occasionally came to volunteer in the classroom. They would help with an art project or read a story during library time. But now, parents are being asked to help out even more. If we want our kids to have everything we had growing up, we're going to need to chip in and help raise funds to make it happen. If you had told me that P.E., art, music, and library were not part of an elementary school education, I would have been shocked. School booster clubs have to raise money for these "basics" that the school district now thinks of merely as "extras."

Fundraising is a tough, but rewarding job. No matter what fundraising effort you're planning, you need to have a committed group of parents willing to put in the work. It's important to remember that everyone is a *volunteer* and everyone is working toward a common goal. People should be treated well and appreciated! Don't make the mistake of trying to do it all alone. You'll need lots of voices, lots of energy, and lots of stakeholders to join you in your efforts. It takes a village. Parents these days are doing their best to help their kids learn and grow and enjoy a well-rounded education.

This book is structured as a guide to help you plan and navigate through different ways to fundraise for your child's school. It is designed to help you close the gap between what the school district gives and what our children need to succeed. I hope it helps you raise lots of money so you can give your children the education they deserve.

# INTRODUCTION:FUNDRAISING IS LIKE PREPARING A MEAL

Sometimes when you cook, you simply need to make a quick meal for the kids. You can make Mac & Cheese or microwave some fish sticks and broccoli. Both are great solutions if you don't have a lot of time but you want to make sure your kids are happy and full.

At other times, you may want to prepare a little fancier dish- i.e. a roast chicken with vegetables. This takes a little bit more planning, a little more thought, and a little more time and effort. Hopefully, that extra effort is appreciated and enjoyed. Your family will know that you put a little love into the meal.

Then there are times when you want to pull off a gourmet masterpiece for 12 guests. Perhaps you're having friends over with their kids or you're throwing a dinner party for some people from the office. If you're trying to impress someone, you can bet the meal will take extra time and preparation. It's pretty rare that I invite someone into my home for a meal and I serve something microwaved. I want my guests to feel special and appreciated. I want them to know that they are worth the extra effort and I'm glad to have them in my home.

No matter what meal you're serving, each type of meal has its own merits. The meal simply has to fit the occasion. We occasionally have friends over for Sunday brunch. Most of the time I try to make a quiche with homemade dough. Sometimes I use the pre-made dough. Sometimes I just go to the bagel store and serve bagels- all I have to do is toast them and let my guests dress them up with cream cheese or other extras! There's no shame in that. We all do it, and a bagel breakfast is often just as satisfying as the homemade quiche or soufflé.

You have to think about whom you're feeding. Kids will respond differently to a meal than adults. Friends from the office may have higher expectations than the parents of your child's best playmate. Each meal has to work for your needs and for the audience you are feeding.

Some meals can be created on your own and sometimes cooking requires a few extra hands helping in the kitchen. The amount of kitchen support depends on the expectation level you're setting for your meal. If you do want to involve others, you can have one child chop the veggies for the salad and another paint the sauce on the chicken. Everyone feels good about what they contribute to the meal and takes pride in what they've done to help. And if the kids have a sense of ownership about what you're making, they will be more invested in the meal's success.

Preparing a successful fundraiser is just like preparing a successful meal. Some projects will take a long time to get up and running and will require a lot of hands, while others are a faster turnaround with not too much effort. As we go through the different fundraising opportunities in this book, I will compare them with typical meal preparations. I'll try and show you what you need to do to shop, prep, and cook and ultimately set the table for a successful meal. I will share with you how to figure out the expense involved, the tools you'll need, the number of people who need to be involved in the preparation and execution of your fundraiser and how much time it will take. I'll also try to show you how much money your fundraiser might bring in (though that is completely dependent on your school community). Hopefully, this book will help you find new strategies for fundraising while getting a better handle on what is required before your pot starts to boil over.

## SETTING THE TABLE: THINGS YOU WILL WANT TO KNOW BEFORE YOU GET STARTED

Identify What You Need To Fundraise For
Know Your Audience
Create A Clear Message
Determine How To Get Your Message Out
*Do you have letterhead and a logo?*
*Do you have your nonprofit status?*
Set Up A Calendar

If you are at a school that has never done any kind of fundraising before, you will want to look at this section to make sure you have basic things you will need.

**Identify What You Need to Fundraise For:** Ask yourself this very important question: *Why do you need to fundraise for your school?* It's a serious question. The answer is different from state to state and it's different from school to school. Some schools raise money for Art Programs, Music, P.E. or Library. Others focus on Media Lab or Science. There are plenty of schools in California that try to raise money to provide downsizing teachers so the kids can have smaller class sizes, which makes for a more manageable learning environment.

Schools with predominantly lower income student populations get Title I funds...and those funds can be significant. Title 1 schools are often equipped with top of the line computers and smart boards in the classroom. These schools usually aren't hurting for cash to bring in technology and personnel. However, these schools have other needs.

At one of the lower income schools in Los Angeles, they give out bread three times a week for families who don't have food. Families line up after school to get the donated food to provide for their families.

A former assistant principal at one of these predominantly lower-income schools was only able to recall one fundraiser at his school. At his school there was more effort spent on getting the kids excited about learning and coming to school. Popcorn and ice cream was given out to students who didn't miss a day in a month. T-shirts that encouraged the kindergartners to learn their sight words were given out to each student who could read all the site words.

If you don't have your school's needs clearly defined, it makes it much harder to get people excited about participating. Remember, any fundraising program should always put the kids and their needs first.

**Know Your Audience:** You have to know your audience. Just as you wouldn't ask families at a low-income school to donate $10,000 each, you wouldn't send a request out to a predominantly Spanish speaking community in English. If your parent population were primarily renters and not homeowners, you wouldn't use the selling point that making this school better helps your property values go up. That won't speak to your audience. The better you know your audience, the more successful any appeal will be.

**Create A Clear Message:** The approach, *the way in which you ask for money*, is different depending on your school. You want to craft your message so it gets the best response. It's important to show how a donor's contribution will directly impact your child's school experience. You can do this by making the problem important to the people you are asking for money. Try to explain the problem in one sentence or less: ex. *There is no money in the district budget for a P.E. coach and it is so important for our children to learn healthy habits for the rest of their lives.* Then give them the one sentence solution: *The money we raise with this walkathon will allow us to hire a PE Coach.*

**Determine How To Get Your Message Out:** What are the best ways for you to communicate to your audience? Does your school have a website? Does your school send information home in backpacks or do they communicate primarily by email to the parents? Do they put up home made signs on the fences to let the parent-body know what's going on or does the Principal do a phone blast that calls all the parents to let them know what is happening in the school community each week? It is important to know how your school communicates with the parents and find out what works best for your school.

**Letterhead & Logos**: An elementary school should look professional too. Any letters you send out asking for donations should be on school or booster club letterhead. The logo doesn't have to be stuffy and corporate. It can have some whimsy to it. But remember: you are sending a request to ask for a donation or a contribution and you want to be taken seriously- it's important to show your potential donors that you're serious.

**Nonprofit Status**: Does your booster club or fundraising organization have a 501c3 tax ID number (non profit status)? The 501c3 is a federal tax ID that allows anyone who donates to the organization to get a tax write off. Aside from providing a benefit to your contributors, a tax ID # lets your donors know that you are part of a professional organization. The National PTA provides all of its member schools with their nonprofit status and appropriate paperwork. If your school doesn't have a booster club or an existing 501c3 status, look to PTA as an easy way to get the process started.

**Set Up A Calendar:** Finally, before you get started, create a calendar and decide what fundraisers you want to do and when. Don't put yourself in the position of having to constantly ask for donations. If your audience feels like they are being "hit up" for money all the time, they will become desensitized and turn off. They will not give.

Make sure you aren't doing too much in a short period. For example, you may not want to do a Thanksgiving and Christmas appeal because they are so close together. Many schools celebrate the 100th day of school (the school year is typically 180 days so 100 marks a little more than the halfway point; there is also educational benefit in encouraging the kids to talk about the number 100). Some schools plan a fundraiser associated with the 100th day of school. If you decide to do a big fundraiser for Valentine's Day, you may discover that it's awfully close to the 100th day. Don't schedule two fundraisers around the same time and make parents choose which fundraiser to give to. If giving opportunities are spaced out enough over the course of the year, parents are less likely to get donor fatigue.

There is a lot to think about when you decide to take on fundraising for your child's school. There are a lot of factors that need to be considered, and a lot of people will need to be involved to make a difference. But there are very few parents out in the world who don't want their kids to have the best education they can possibly have.

## MAKING THE INVITATIONS: HOW TO GET PEOPLE AND BUSINESSES INVOLVED

Depending on the type of fundraisers you hope to do, you're almost always going to have to ask businesses for donations. These items can range from small things like a dinner for two at a local restaurant to larger things like donating a car for a raffle. The ASK, or *how you request a donation*, is important. Local businesses are more than happy to donate if you ask them…but you have to ask. They will not offer it.

Think of asking as like making an invitation. When you plan an event, you create an invitation. You aren't going to get engraved invitations for a backyard BBQ, and you probably wouldn't use evite to invite people to a wedding. Different events require different approaches.

Similarly, different types of events require different types of donations:

For an auction, you will want to get gift cards or certificates to restaurants and hopefully package them with tickets to the theatre or the movies. For the Walk-a-thon, you may want to ask the local grocery store to donate flats of water. Finding a great raffle prize can take some time and effort. Think of what you would want to win: an iPad? a flat screen TV? cash? This is when your letter writing skills will come in handy. You'll need to reach out to the businesses in your community and ask for what you want. There are so many different ways to approach possible contributors.

If you are organized in your process, it will make everything that much easier. Here are the seven key steps to consider when setting out to get items or events donated to your school. Make sure you have your message and all the tools we discussed in the last section before trying to take on this larger step.

## THE SEVEN STEPS IN SETTING UP AN EFFECTIVE GET SQUAD

1. Research and Be Prepared
2. Be Creative When Deciding What You Want To Get
3. Get A Team Together- Create Your Very Own "Get Squad"
4. Be Happy & Positive
5. Just Ask
6. Sell, Sell, Sell
7. Follow-up

**Research and Be Prepared:** You need to be organized. You need to know whom you've sent letters and emails to and you need to follow up. At my school, we used a simple excel spreadsheet to keep close tabs on the status of our donation requests. I've spoken to many parents that utilized Google docs or classroom websites to share information. But you have to have the information codified and organized in one location.

*Know What You Are Looking For:* It's important to know what you're looking for. This is usually a function of what people in your community are interested in. If you live in a community where it gets really hot, getting an air conditioning company to donate service calls is a great idea. But you wouldn't want to get a snow blower donated if you live somewhere where it never snows.

*Make it easy to ask and easier to give:* It's a good idea for anyone who is going to be asking for donations to carry ad and donation forms with them wherever they go. This eliminates delays in asking for donations and reduces effort in following up. It's also a good idea to have many different ways that a business can donate. For example, maybe your school could print a local business directory. Starting at $50, businesses can advertise their support of the school in the directory. Or perhaps a restaurant doesn't want to donate a gift certificate but they could provide free meals to your volunteers during event preparation. It's always good to give businesses many different ways they can participate.

*Learn from your school's history*: If your school has held fundraisers with donated items in the past, it's always helpful to review what items were donated in the past and how popular they were. Hopefully, whoever was responsible for obtaining those items kept records to show how much money different kinds of donations yielded.

After any event, you should determine whether the work involved in getting the donation yielded good results. If, for example, it took weeks or months of calling and writing to get a beauty basket worth $500 from a company and it only made $20, or worse – it didn't sell at all, you may want to rethink spending so much time on getting that item the following year.  On a larger scale, you need to consider how much time you are putting in to the event, and how much it is making.

After the auction, you should determine how much items sold for. "Restaurants" typically make at least 90-100% (or more) of their value, while "Health, fitness, and beauty" donations will usually go for around 40-50% at best.  You'll want to get some of those items again regardless of what they brought in.

You may be able to get an abundance of photography sittings, haircuts, piano lessons and karate classes.  Limit the amount you use in an auction. You don't want to offer too many similar items because it reduces the potential for competitive bidding. It's important to know what your school community likes and what they want.  Are the parents more interested in art camp for the kids or botox for themselves? Would they enjoy tickets to a rock concert, or a Broadway show?  The great thing about auctions is there is usually something for everyone.

*Ask the right person*: Make sure when asking for a donation, that you know who to talk to. If seeking a donation from a business or storefront, always speak to the owner or manager. Most salespeople don't have the authority to make donations. Remember to express your appreciation no matter what size the donation is. ALL donations are tax deductible.

**Be Creative:** If you're willing to think outside the box, there's no limit to the number and diversity of things you can get donated. Every auction gets restaurant donations and karate classes. But the schools that get palm readings, poker parties, and termite inspections donated really raise the bar. It may seem crazy to ask someone to donate termite inspection but if your community is made up primarily of homeowners, you can bet someone is going to need that inspection at some point.

*Take Advantage of Your Neighborhood*: Think about what you have in your town or city. In Los Angeles, there are opportunities like The Hollywood Bowl or studio tours. You need to think about what YOU like and you can probably come up with some great ideas. There are great items under your nose: We all have special talents and connections…in most cases people just need to be given the idea. So ask around and find unusual items to get donated. Here are just a few:

Vacation Homes
Theatre/Music Tickets
Frequent Flyer Miles
Lessons (tennis, piano, singing, cooking, knitting)
Art Work
Sporting Events
Memorabilia (sports, music, etc)
Architectural Walking Tours
A gourmet dinner cooked for your family
Summer Camps

*Sometimes the best things in life are free!* Look at some ways to make money from nothing! When I started, we added a couple of cost-free items to the silent auction: We asked the Principal if we could recognize kids birthdays on the school marquee one week each month. We also asked if he would allow a student to join him during his daily all-school loud-speaker announcements. It was revenue we tapped into that was created from nothing. It costs the school nothing to add a Happy Birthday message to the marquee…and the school got at least $100 for one each month.

The same approach worked with the morning announcements. That's more than $2000 that wasn't gotten before. It adds up, and every little bit helps. Some schools do

VIP seats for graduations and holiday performances. There's also coveted parking spots. That will add even more. What about naming the auditorium or cafeteria or library for the year? It never hurts to ask. The Get Squad motto is: "You can't get, if you don't ask." This is all free money. If your school administration will let you take advantage of it, the amount you can raise is unlimited!

**Creating a Get Squad:** It's so important to have a team of positive, enthusiastic people who want to help and make a difference. The Get Squad was a fun name I came up with for getting items donated for our silent auction.

Before I was at my daughter's school, the team of parents that got items for the annual auction and dinner dance was called "procurement." This never sounded right to me. While they had success getting items and raising money, changing the name provided a great conversation starter and made the experience of the ASK less clinical and formal and more exciting and engaging.

The people who run your Get Squad or solicit donations should be outgoing and not afraid to ask. Ask what? Just Ask. For anything. You cannot get anything unless you ask.

Communicate with your team and lead them through each step in the process. Give them the tools they need to go out and do the job, and watch them fly! If you show them what to do and how to do it at the very start of the process, it will be so much easier for them to understand the job and also be able to do it. Remind everyone that everything we do, we do for our kids. Tell the volunteers not to be afraid to ASK for help if they feel lost or confused.

Remind your team that communication is a two-way street. Have your team email with updates each week. They should let you know what they've gotten and the status of the item. They should also let you know if they're having trouble with a particular donor. If you can use these updates as a way to build enthusiasm and celebrate successes together, your team will be stronger day by day.

**Be Happy & Positive:** Whether you decide to head up the Get Squad team, or be one of the team members, it is important to be happy and positive. Every time you are asking for a contribution, whether from a fellow parent or from a local business, you are representing the school. Nobody wants to give to unpleasant people. Donors want to know how their participation is making the school a better place, not how bad it is. If you stay positive, your response is more likely to be positive.

**Just Ask**: Don't be afraid to ask – at restaurants where you dine, places where your kids take classes, theatres, movies, shops. Most places are happy to donate. Whenever we would go out for dinner, my husband would just stand back and watch me work. I'd always ask to speak to the Manager. When he or she came over, I would compliment the meal and explain that I am getting items and gift certificates for the local public school. In most cases, people were HAPPY to oblige. I would walk into meat markets and super markets and bring the letter with our 501c3 and they would happily comply! You see, even in a tough economy, all you have to do is ask.

Don't forget: *Businesses want customers!* A donation serves them as an advertisement for their business. At an auction, your guests will see their donation and want to bid on it. One person will win it, but the rest are potential new customers. They know the business supports the school and that, in turn, makes them want to support the business. Word of mouth shouldn't be underestimated. New customers could tell more people and suddenly, a business that is struggling, may start to turn around…all because of one donation!

Some people will make a donation on their own, but most people need a little nudge. Some people will say no. Don't let it discourage you. You need to be diligent and vigilant. Rest assured, it is a great feeling when you get a donation that was hard-won.

**Sell, Sell, Sell**: Remind potential donors that their business will be seen by all the families whose children go to your school (if you can provide the numbers, that is usually meaningful for them. You'll likely want to list donors in program books, next to their donations or with signs or banners. If you want, you can also create placards for their store windows, which will give them GREAT exposure and provides good will. Donors are not purely altruistic. If you can show them how this donation will help them, they will be more likely to give.

**Have I mentioned FOLLOW UP?:** Sometimes businesses need time to make decisions. You can fill out some of the form for them and let them know you will follow up (make a note to yourself to follow up each week). You can also email the owner and attach forms for them. Don't make a donor have to find the right website, forms, or how to donate. The more you can make their donating process smooth and easy, the more likely they will be to give.

Occasionally, an item will fall through the cracks simply because nobody knew they needed to go and pick it up. If you're keeping a list of items with their status, you shouldn't run into this problem. If your efforts are organized, your team communicative, and your positive energy infectious, you will avoid common pitfalls. Following-up combines all of these skills. It can be the key to making sure your efforts yield the results you're hoping for.

Unless you get a definite no – KEEP TRYING! In some instances, a person will tell you they need to get approval and you won't hear back either because they forgot or didn't get approval. Call again...weekly. They'll usually be glad you called to remind them.

Working on The Get Squad requires a lot of follow up calling, e-mailing and sometimes, stopping in to remind the businesses who you are and why you are trying to get their help. Until you get a no, you can stay on them like a rodeo rider on a bull.

## SAMPLE PITCHES

I have included sample scripts and letters that you can use to help you with your fundraising. These letters work, but often they are only the first step in a process. Don't assume that every donation will just start rolling in the day after you send out the letters. Many solicitations by mail require follow-up: by email, by phone, or even in person. So don't make the mistake of thinking that once your letters are in the mail you're done. You're really just getting started.

These letters are specific to my school and what we needed and who our parents are. You need to change it to fit your school's needs and the community around you.

A letter for a raffle item might look something like this:

*Dear _____,*

*My name is Sarah Barrett and I'm a parent volunteer working to make my daughters' school just a little bit better. Every year, we hold a raffle that raises money for Art and Science teachers for the school. I know that Apple gives quite a bit of money to educational endeavors, including schools. We have received grants from you to get computers for our Media Lab in the past. We would love to be able to raffle off an iPad for our fall fundraiser. The event is in six months, so I am hoping that will give you plenty of time to say yes (a girl can dream, can't she?).*

*I have included information about our school and what our fundraising efforts have been able to do in the past few years. Any support that you can give us would be so appreciated. Thank you for your consideration and for all you are doing to help the children of today be the innovators of tomorrow!*

*Sincerely,*

For an auction item, you may want to go into more detail about what the fundraising is for. It might look like this.

The text in brackets should be customized for your needs...you can change that part.

*Hi _____,*

*My name is [Sarah Barrett] and I am a parent volunteer working on our annual auction and dinner dance.*

*Thank you so much for passing this on to [American Girl Corporate] for me. Our public school, [Carpenter Community Charter] is part of the [Los Angeles Unified School District], and we are one of the top schools in our neighborhood. We are still in dire need of money to keep some of the wonderful enrichment we provide for our students -- art, science, computers, dance and physical education. The money we raise at our annual auction and dinner dance helps continue these programs.*

*Attached please find a copy of the donation letter for [our school]. The event is on_____, and we are doing a big push for auction items over the next 8 weeks. I know you need the 8-week lead time, so I'm hoping this will work out!*

*We would love to get something from [American Girl] -- Here are some ideas of what we would love to have...I know this is a lot, but I'm reaching for the stars, in hopes that Corporate will give us one or some of these:*

*1. A Birthday Party*
*2. Lunch or Afternoon Tea for 4*
*3. Tickets to one of your shows*
*4. An American Girl Gift Card*
*5. A doll and matching clothes for the child*

*Of course any donation would be wonderful and is 100% tax deductible.*

*Thank you so much for supporting our school. We know you probably get a lot of requests, and your help is most appreciated!*

*Thanks,*

24

Here's a sample approach for a simpler ask. In the letter below, we are trying to get a straightforward gift certificate for a free dinner at a local restaurant. If you had carried a donation form in your purse, you wouldn't have had to send this email. But perhaps you could send a letter like this as follow-up to a donation form. Either way, it's always helpful to let the potential donor know that you're also a client.

Hi _____,

My friend and I had the pleasure of eating at [Sweetsalt] the other day! It was fabulous!! We'd love it if you would consider donating something for our big school fundraiser. A gift card or a party for 10 would be fantastic!! [School name here] is a public school in [LA Unified] and we have been hit very hard by the cuts they are making. The money raised at the auction will help keep programs like P.E., Science, Dance, and Computers going so that our kids get a well-rounded education.

I am attaching the donation form for you. Please let me know if you have ANY questions! I look forward to eating at your restaurant again soon...and hope to have you as part of our auction!

Best,
Sarah Barrett
Parent Volunteer and dedicated Mom
[Add your contact info here]

## PHONE SCRIPT FOR BUSINESSES WHO HAVE DONATED PREVIOUSLY

*Hi, my name is _____ and I'm a parent volunteer for _____ school. I know you've been generous in donating to our annual auction in the past, and I'm hoping we can count on your support again this year. I'd be happy to email you the forms or drop them off – whatever is easier for you. Every dollar raised goes toward the enrichment programs like PE, Science, Dance, Computers, and Music. This is one of the reasons that our school is one of the best public schools in Los Angeles. We are hoping you will donate items (like you did last year). All donations are tax deductible and we will be sending out those tax letters after the event. I will call you next week to follow up. Thank you so much for taking the time, and for your continuous support of the school.*

## PHONE SCRIPT FOR BUSINESSES WHO HAVE NOT DONATED

*Hi, my name is _____and I'm a parent volunteer for _____ school in (your city). We are a public school – with LA Unified, and though we have gotten Charter status, we still have to raise money every year to support the enrichment classes that the school district doesn't cover. We have done an auction and dinner dance for the past [22 years] and with the money raised, our kids are able to have PE, Science, Computer Lab, Music and Dance. Donating to our school is a way to get your company in front of your target audience. It would be great exposure for you because we have over [700 families] at the school and they are VERY supportive of businesses that support the school. This is an inexpensive way for you to get publicity and reach out to the audience your business wants to attract. Many of our parents are educated, upper-middle class families who enjoy dining, shopping, travelling and other unique experiences. There are many ways to donate. You can donate an item or gift certificate and you can also become a*

*Partner in Education (PIE) with a cash donation. Every donation is tax deductible and goes a long way to improving our children's education.*

## RESPONSE IF THEY SAY NO
*Yes, I realize that the economy has made businesses rethink their bottom line, but this is cheaper than advertising and you are attracting a huge amount of people who actually will shop and support your business. All that, and it is tax deductible!! It's a win-win for everyone!*

## ADDED VALUE ITEMS
*Donations to the booster club are tax deductible
*Donors receive a school supporter placard to hang in their window or by the cash register or check-in area. This is important for their business – parents shop at businesses that support the school.

# BEHAVIORAL EMAIL MARKETING MESSAGE FOR PARENTS

A quick note about what this letter is, before you read it. I have a friend who makes a living by doing email marketing. Mike Michalowicz is a marketing guru who manages a website called The Toilet Paper Entrepreneur. Mike's behavioral email marketing messages are designed for businesses, but they can be used just as effectively to raise money for your child's school, soccer club, or swim team.

These messages are different in several ways. First, they create a sense of "us." The message is personalized and helps connect the reader with the writer and provides a sense of their shared responsibility and experience. Think about this: When you look at a political candidate, do you trust the person who says "You need to have lower taxes and stronger education," or the person who says "**We** need to have lower taxes and stronger education?" We all want to trust the person who sounds like they are in it with us. We are a team and together, we can fix the problems.

Secondly, it is important to send the letter via email. Emailing allows the reader to respond right away...with one click of the mouse, they can take action. They can let you know about a donation they can make or offer to help by volunteering. With a letter that comes home in backpacks, you have to hope that your parents actually (a) get it, (b) don't place it in a "to do" pile, and (c) don't find it days later crumpled at the bottom of the backpack with a half eaten granola bar. This is a more personalized and emotional letter and it's also more informal.

Finally, it is so important to ask directly for what you want in these letters. You need help...let the reader know this. Put it in your subject line. By asking for help, you are giving the reader (other parents) an opportunity to be part of the solution. Sometimes just letting the parents know HOW they can help gets you the results you need. With an email, all your parents have to do is hit "reply" and let someone know you can help in some small way. They will want to be invested in helping their kids' school, because ultimately, it benefits their kids!

The email messages should be quick, easy and to the point. They let the parents know who you are (that you are a parent – just like them) and that you need their help. It should be direct and friendly. You want to let the parents know who you are and how you came to be involved. Most importantly, you need to come right out and <u>ask for their help</u>. Use names wherever you can...it makes it more personal and gives your audience another way to connect. Include an attachment of or a link to the donation form, so they can print it out right away and donate something!

It also helps to give your prospective donors a short time frame so they take action right away- i.e. "I need to hear from you in the next 3 days, so I can start 'hitting the phones'." This works! I have used this technique the past few years and it always yields results! It can be used in fundraising of all kinds...sports teams, schools and more.

See the letter below:

*Dear (school) Families,*

*I want to thank you for being part of the [school] Community!*

*My [daughter, Emily, is a student here in 2nd grade]. I gladly volunteered to coordinate getting donations for the school's silent auction and dinner dance when [the co-chairs of the event – use their names] asked me.*

*I am reaching out to you because I'm seeking your help for [school]. Unfortunately due to the economic climate, some past supporters have gone out of business or can no longer donate or sponsor our biggest fundraiser of the year. We need support in order to keep the incredible programs [Science, Computers, Dance, PE, Music – not to mention lowering class sizes in 4th and 5th grades] our children participate in every day.*

*I want to see if you can join me in contributing to the event. Donations of any amount are tax deductible! Every* *little bit helps: if you go to a restaurant or take your child to an art class, all you have to do is **ask** for a donation! The worst they can say is no, but the best case scenario will mean money for the school – money that is needed to help our children become well-rounded individuals. The benefits for the kids are numerous.*

*Please just drop me an email back and tell me if you would be interested in donating and I will get all the details to you immediately. You can also get a donation form in the main office or by clicking this link:*

*{You should set up a link that can be accessed on the school website and put here.}*

*If you cannot donate, I fully understand. Please know that either way, I am thrilled your child is an active member of [school]. I can't wait to see you at the Auction and Dinner Dance on [insert date].*

*Thank you!!!*

*P.S. Please email me back in the next three days, since we need to start "hitting the phones" by Monday.*
*Sarah Barrett (phone #)*
*The Get Squad Team Captain*
*your clickable email goes here*

This type of letter accomplishes two things: (1) It gives parents an opportunity to help and (2) it tells them exactly how to do it. Parents typically want to help but they don't because they don't know how. With this letter, you are reaching out to them directly and asking them to help. You're also giving them specific instructions about how they can help and giving them all the tools they need to act immediately. Even if only a few parents respond, it's a great tool. It may bring in new people who have never been involved before. You may be able to reach out to people who have never felt able to help or known how to help. And when you're fundraising, every little bit helps!

## TEN BASIC RULES OF FUNDRAISING... NOT NECESSARILY IN THIS ORDER

1. Know your message
2. Know your audience
3. Make what you're asking for as clear as possible.
4. Ask Politely
5. Follow-up
6. Don't give up
7. Send Thank You notes
8. Show people how they have made a difference
9. Build relationships with businesses
10. Have fun!

# SECTION 1: THE MOST IMPORTANT FUNDRAISING PROGRAMS AKA THE BIG MEALS: HOW TO FEED YOUR SCHOOL

In Section 1, we'll review the biggest fundraisers for the school. These programs bring in the most money and generally require a group of people to work together in order for a successful outcome. The fundraisers in this section will be those that typically make the most money. If you break it down into pieces and share the work with a good group of volunteers, it will feel much more manageable.

## ANNUAL GIFT DONATIONS

Most schools have some version of an Annual Gift Campaign. They ask parents to donate a certain amount of money per child as their annual gift to the school. I've seen amounts vary from $200 -$1,000 per child in public schools and sometimes even more in private schools. This is a suggested donation – not a requirement. Some parents will donate more, some will donate less, and some will not donate at all. Set a goal for how much you want to raise. The number you settle on should be based on the assumption that 35-50% of parents will contribute. If you have more buy-in, good for you!

Proceeds from the Annual Gift Drive may help cover costs of supplies in the classroom and field trips; the funds might also be used to fund extra teachers to reduce the size of a class or to bring in music or art specialists. Some schools ask for a lower financial contribution and then require you to bring in all sorts of supplies for the classroom – paper, rulers, pencils, wipes, paper towels, etc. Some schools include classroom funds in their campaign so parents only have to write one check and won't have to worry about classroom specific items throughout the year (yearbook, teacher gift, field trips, etc.). The way an Annual Campaign is designed varies widely from school to school. As long as you know what you're asking for and you communicate it effectively to your parents, you should have no problem.

At one school, the parents who donate the suggested amount get a tile that goes on the wall of the school as recognition for all to see. It stays on the wall for years to come. Other schools give car magnets or license plate frames so donors can show their school pride as they're driving around the neighborhood.

Four Easy Steps:
1. Develop the campaign
2. Send something out via mail or in backpacks
3. Remind people with emails or phone calls
4. Recognize those who have contributed.

In terms of prep work for this fundraiser, you will need to come up with a campaign for the year and some marketing to go with it.  You will need to create a donation form and letter.  A great Annual Gift Chair should start talking about the campaign in the first week of school. A really great Chair might also reach out to new parents (kindergarten, especially) over the summer.  Some of these parents may be accustomed to paying a lot for preschool and the "ask" won't feel like a lot to them.

The cooking time on this is basically sending out the letters (either in backpacks or beginning of the year packets) and maybe setting up a few days at tables on campus for questions.  There will be those parents who do stuff right away and those that need a little nudge.  If your school sends email blasts, always include a blurb about your annual donation request.  Without fail, our school did this and each time it was mentioned, a check came in.

As the school year continues, you may need to come up with more creative ways to encourage participation. At our school, the team created a campaign asking parents to give up one thing once a week.  If you gave up one "Tall" Starbucks drink once a week and gave it to the school instead, we would raise $160 per person. Even more if you give up your weekly "Grande" or "Venti!!"

It was a good campaign.  Almost 50% of the community gave that year.  But they still wanted to get the other 50% on board. How? Why didn't they give? For some, it was a financial hardship. For others, they didn't think public school should cost them anything. For others still, they wanted to give, but didn't feel like they could give enough since they couldn't do the suggested minimum...so they didn't give at all.

The following year, the team went to extreme lengths to educate the school community and let them know that they should give what they can. The important part was giving...not the amount. Everyone who donated any amount by December 1st got a car magnet. The Campaign Chairs created a "giving tree" with last names of parents who gave something to the Annual Giving Campaign. 76% gave! That was a HUGE success.

Telling parents to just give what they can could have backfired. They could have ended up making less money with more donors, but they didn't. They became more inclusive and it created a more positive feeling on campus. Would it be great to get the other 24%? Yes, but the growth shown in just one year gave everyone hope.

In Hawaii, one of the school's paddling clubs gives each team member 10 pre-written letters and 10 blank envelopes. Team members are expected to take the envelopes and write addresses of friends and family on them, put a stamp on it and then return all ten addressed, stamped and stuffed envelopes to the canoe club. The club crosses the family's name off the list and then mails them out. It's easy for all involved. The letters are asking friends and family to support by sending in a check to the club.

At a small private school on Maui, their Annual Campaign coordinators get help from a few volunteers who they call "team captains." Each team captain is given a binder that they are expected to circulate to a handful of families. The first family to get the binder is asked to make a donation. They can either put the donation into an envelope, seal it and place it in the back inside pocket of the binder or they can bring their donation to the school office. Once they have made their contribution, the family is supposed to notify the team captain that they've made their contribution and personally pass the binder on to the next family on the list.

This continues until everyone on the list has donated. The expectation is set that every family should donate something, even if only a small amount. The team captain simply has to make sure that each family participates in some way. The secret of this program's success is the way in which they've made "the ask" so deeply personal. The school has nearly 100% participation.

As you can see from the example above, finding a way to encourage parents to communicate and interact is a key element in any successful annual gift campaign. You cannot rely on the letter and marketing alone. At many schools, annual gift chairs follow up their letter with a phone-a-thon. This allows parents to have personal conversations about why they give and encourages greater engagement, involvement, and enthusiasm for your school. Typically, parent volunteers spend two or three nights calling families who have yet to give.

The prep work for this can be as simple as collecting the school directory and marking off each family that has already donated. You will want to have a core group of people making calls in one place (if possible). It's best to make calls in the evening when you know people will be home, and get food for the volunteers so they know they are appreciated as well.

Over several evenings, parents call fellow parents from the school office. Generally, they go down an alphabetical list of parents who have yet to participate in the campaign. You might want to ask 4th grade parents to call fellow 4th grade parents. You might want to divide your list by geographic neighborhoods. You want to set it up so people will welcome the phone call and want to contribute.

If parents say they will give, the volunteers can ask them if they'd like to pay by credit card now or when we can expect payment. This helps the team estimate anticipated income from the campaign and helps give a gentle reminder to parents to give. Get a bell to ring when you get a yes. It keeps the spirits high while you're making calls. Obviously, you will want the volunteers to keep information they collect private. No one needs to know which parent was rude and who refused to pay.

Here's a good example of how a conversation between an Annual Gift Team Member and a parent might go:

*AGT Member: Hi, I'm calling with the [school name] Annual Gift Campaign. I see that you donated last year, but we haven't gotten anything from you yet. Budget cuts with the school district are getting worse every year. Can we count on your support again this year?*
*Parent: I plan to donate again, but can't until January.*
*AGT Member: Would you like us to make a note of it and call you again in January? If it's easier, you can do monthly installments with a credit card.*
*Parent: If you can call to remind me in January, I'd appreciate it. I'm hoping to do the full amount, but not sure if I will be able to do that this year.*
*AGT Member: Whatever you can do would be so appreciated. Thank you so much for supporting the school. We will get in touch with you in January.*

As with any telemarketing/sales campaign, some people will be nice and some people won't be. It will help that you are both parents at the school, but sometimes people are going to be rude and will not want to talk to you. You should try to let it roll off your back and chalk it up to them having a bad day. Any money you get from the calls is a success!

At a school in Portland, Oregon they encourage annual gift donations with something they call a Flamingo Flocking Fun-Raiser. It's one of the most creative forms of "follow-up" I've heard about.

A group of coordinators known as "the flockers" put a flock of plastic flamingos on a family's front lawn for 24 hours. When the pink plastic birds appear on a family's lawn, the parents know that they are being reminded to donate money to the school. It's a fun game. Kids can come with the flockers to help. Once you're part of a "flocked family" the kids can help decorate the flamingos before they leave their house and go on to the next family.

There is a list of families who have agreed to be flocked. The list gets split up by the flockers. There are 10 flockers (they never get flocked) who donate their time and flock other families. Each family will get 7 flamingos placed on their front lawn at night and attached to one of the birds, is a donation form and instructions. The flamingos stay on your lawn for 24 hours. Families who have been flocked bring the donation into the school (no set amount) and can leave a note on the flamingos suggesting another friend to flock. If nobody is suggested, the flocker simply goes to the next family on their list.

Kids talk about the experience at school and wear stickers that say "I've been flocked." It brings a sense of whimsy and fun to the school and helps to encourage community, participation, and donations.

## PARTNERS IN EDUCATION/COMMUNITY SPONSORSHIP

This is a program to encourage businesses (large and small) to make a financial contribution to support your school's programs. For a cash donation, they receive a banner on the school fence and perhaps one or two email advertisements that get sent to the parent body throughout the year. Restaurants that are community sponsors are also encouraged to host special events and/or participate in existing events at the school.

At our school, there are different levels of participation. The lowest is $500 and the highest is $2500+. Consider your community and what levels might be appropriate for your restaurant and business owners. With each increased level, the community sponsors get more exposure to the community, and the school benefits from the cash. For example, a $500 sponsor may be on a banner with 3-4 other companies, while the higher paying sponsors get their own exclusive banner. Companies that pay even more get an advertisement in one or two email blasts that go out to the community and so on.

The prep on this includes creating and updating forms and letters. Try to find new businesses to bring in as well as new ways to build on what and whom you already have.

Think creatively…and outside the box, if you can. You should have a group of parents who are comfortable public speakers going out and meeting the business owners in the community.

It doesn't matter what your school calls it, but when you build your school up by getting the businesses in the community involved, it's a win-win for everyone! Property values go up because people want to live in a neighborhood that has a great school. Businesses feel good because people in the neighborhood are coming to their stores and buying. The school feels good because they are getting the support they need from the community to succeed.

This program looks different at different schools. Some schools put banners up for a certain cash donation to the school. There was a parent at one school who suggested that even though the banners with business names went up in July, new businesses would still be able to get a banner if they donated by November 1st. It's never too late to bring a new donor on board.

Other schools give out signs to hang in business' windows so everyone can see that they are a business that supports the local school. Others do a directory to let parents know what businesses are supporting the school so they can in turn support those businesses. The message is simple: If your community businesses feel invested in your school, your community will become tighter, stronger, and more unified. And that, in turn, leads to stronger more sustainable educational environments for our kids.

## THE PARTY BOOK

The Party Book is a fundraiser that allows you to bring your school community together. Different parents and/or teachers volunteer to host parties and then other parents can sign up online to attend these fun events. There is a per person or per couple or per family charge for each event and 100% of the money goes to your school. The people who host the events as well as attendees can write off the parties as a tax deduction.

There are events for kids, some for families and some just for adults. The idea is to have parties that your community members would attend anyway. Using the Party Book, parents pay to participate and then meet new people in your school community while donating to the school. One school I know has a teacher who loves hiking. She donates hikes on set dates. Anyone who wants to go, signs up through the online party book, pays their money and goes!

There is some prep work involved in this project. I've seen it done by a huge team of people and I've seen it done by just two people. Traditionally, party book events were advertised using physical books that listed lots of events and then the books were photocopied and distributed to all the parents. This is not a very "green" approach. It can also be a lot of work and might end up being a logistical nightmare when it comes to collecting money for the parties.

Now you can put your Party Book online. The online system works very well since it records who is attending, collects payment, and provides all the information on an easily viewable website. Each party planner can look online and know who is coming to the party and if it is getting full. Potential guests can see who else is going to the party. If you want to maintain privacy for people participating in the events or limit participation to just your parents at your particular school, the site can require passwords for all participants.

One of the easiest online Party Book programs is called the Online Party Book (www.onlinepartybook.com). There is a $500 fee to put the book online, and there are some basic steps you need to take to get things set-up for your school's event. You'll need to establish some rules and procedures for the party hosts so they understand what they can do and what is expected of them as hosts.

You will need people to recruit families to donate parties, someone to do the data entry online and a couple of people to promote and market the parties. The coordinators have to know the school community and ask people to host parties.

Parents can host kid's parties (by grade, by class, or open to anyone), adult parties and family parties. Parties can be for as few as eight people and as many as 100. It is completely up to whatever the host is willing to do.

Parties can be anything from $40 for 4 hikes in the local trails on specific mornings to a BBQ in someone's backyard to an afternoon tea at a local museum or hotel. Themed dinner parties (martini, game night, poker), cooking classes, book clubs, clam bakes, card making parties and massages and martini parties are popular party ideas.

The hosts of each party pay for the events and they get the tax deduction for it. So as an example, you can have a kindergarten parent host a kinder art party for 25 students. You could also have a 5th grade mom plan a party for some of her friends to have a manicurist come for an afternoon and do everyone's nails as they sit in the backyard drinking margaritas. It's all about what each person wants to donate and how many people want to go!

The sky is really the limit with these parties. Here are some of our favorite ideas:

1. Afternoon tea by the sea with the principal
2. Kickball in the park for a couple of grade levels
3. Museum tours given by a parent or teacher expert
4. Yoga class given by a parent expert
5. Gingerbread house decorating party at the holidays
6. Cinco de Mayo Margarita & Mojitos Party
7. Poker party for dads (using gift cards instead of cash)
8. A Scrabble battle or Mah Jong party
9. A progressive Dinner through a neighborhood
10. The No-Drama-Mama Pajama Party

Once parents volunteer to host a party, they will submit a form with information about the party. Hopefully they've written up a description of the event that makes it sound exciting and appealing. If not, you'll need to rewrite the event and make it sound like a great activity- the kind most parents will not want to miss. You also need to create a sense of scarcity. Limit attendance and make sure people understand that they need to sign up quickly so they don't miss out on a really fun night.

Once you've put together a great group of activities, the next step in the process is advertising and promoting the parties and getting people to sign up to participate. You can do many different things to promote the parties: Signs around the school, email blasts, and room parent involvement are all key.

You need to inspire parents to check out the parties online. It is best to set out a calendar of events and post all the parties online at the same time. When you set your launch date, make sure people know about it and make sure they know that some events will sell out quickly. If you do this, you'll have a better chance of driving people to the site as soon as the parties are posted live. This will help to create some buzz around all of the events.

Once the parties start filling up, it's up to you to keep talking about the parties and reminding people of the opportunities on a regular basis. You can send reminders about parties that don't fill up so parents can add their names to the list. If some parties are not selling out, it is the Party Book team's job to find a way to build interest.

If it's a new concept for your community, it may be hard to get people on board. Still, unlike big dinner dance events, this has almost no cost (except that $500). Also, it allows anyone in the community to sign up to go to a party, as opposed to other events that sometimes have an entry price. Anything that opens up your school community and makes it a little more accessible for everyone in the community is great.

The thing I like most about the party book is that it really helps build the community. The school makes money and parents can build lasting friendships and feel more involved. How can it be bad? I know lots of schools that have had HUGE success with The Party Book. Here's the key: if you would pay to go to a dinner or cooking class anyway, by attending the party, you are getting what you would have gotten anyway and the school is benefitting!

You can see samples of party books here:
http://www.onlinepartybook.com/examples.php

# AUCTIONS

Auctions are a great and exciting way to raise money. Simply put, auctions are a public sale of an item to the highest bidder. When you get great items donated to your school, holding an auction is one of the most effective ways to get a high return on investment. The item goes to the highest bidder. Usually you set a timeline for how long the auction will last and then the highest bidder is the winner. This is a fabulous way to raise money for the school and get some great items for yourself or your kids!

The prep work for auctions is enormous. Not only the process of getting items to auction off, but also setting up, organizing the room, creating the atmosphere and checking people in and out. This requires A LOT of people or a lot of money to hire someone to do it. Even if you choose to hire someone, there are a lot of details that parents will need to think about. It's important to build excitement about the items you have.

Auctions are a great way to raise money. It is always best to hold an auction when big groups of parents will be gathering at an event. I've seen and heard about auctions being held during carnivals, Halloween events and as part of dinner dance events. Auctions tend to do better when they are during adult evenings such as a dinner dance. This is because alcohol is likely served and inhibitions are down. People bid more when they are having fun and drinking.

## A. LIVE AUCTIONS

Live auctions are for special items that will draw more interest than your typical items. For example, I know a school that was able to get a few signed guitars from Duran Duran. The school was able to authenticate the signatures and sell the guitars on eBay for thousands of dollars. Another great item people have auctioned is a trip somewhere. People love to travel, and if they can get a bargain, even better. I have known schools that have auctioned off everything from a puppy to Principal for a day!

This past year our school came up with a cooking competition between two dads who like to cook. Neither was a professional chef, but they created the most incredible menu and five couples bid to be judges and attend the dinner. We also were able to auction off 20 spots for the cocktail party before the dinner. That one event raised $4500.

For a live auction, it is important to have a skilled auctioneer- someone who can build excitement and keep the auction moving. It is important to start the pricing at a reasonable starting bid so you have somewhere to go. You don't want to start a bid at $1,000 and end it at $1,100. The excitement level for these items should be high and the auctioneer helps create the atmosphere of excitement.

## B. ONLINE AUCTIONS

Online Auctions are held on the internet and allow people to bid from anywhere. Your great aunt Sylvia can help your child's school by bidding on the hand painted plate your child made in class, or a gift certificate to a chain restaurant that has a location in her city as well as yours. The online auction allows more people to bid (thereby hopefully getting a higher percentage of value on your items) and gives more people the opportunity to get great stuff and write it off as a school donation!

Sometimes online auctions can be less work than a silent auction. I know a lot of schools that have Bidding For Good do their online auctions. Bidding For Good also serves as your Get Squad, obtaining many of the items for the online auction for a fee. The parents sometimes supplement it and typically the more successful online auctions have a high percentage of items that were obtained locally.

When undertaking an online auction, you may need to store items while the auction is going on. This can be a bigger burden than you might realize, especially if you do not plan for it. You will also have to deliver all of the items to whoever bought them, no matter how far away he or she may be.

Depending on the tools you use for your online auction, you need to plan time and resources for shipping the items to the winning bidders.

A lot of schools prefer to do online auctions instead of holding a big event. There are pros and cons to this. The pros are that you can open it up to friends and family to do more bidding and get more people involved in trying to win great stuff. You also don't have the expense of creating a large physical event and bringing people together. Finally, silent auctions can be managed by a smaller team and take a lot less time and energy to organize, so you won't be taxing your volunteers as heavily.

There are also several reasons you may not want to do a silent auction. First and foremost, you lose out on all the benefits of bringing the community together. Online auctions are more impersonal and don't have the excitement and intimacy of a fundraiser that brings people together. Many people also resist an online auction because they like to see and touch the items they're bidding on, not just view a picture on a website. Finally, with online auctions you lose out on the alcohol factor: When people are drinking and having a good time at an event, they bid on more items and buy more stuff. You can't underestimate the value of a bidder who may feel freer with their money.

Ultimately, you'll need to decide if an online auction works for your particular community. If your school has never done an auction before, it might be a good place to start as you'll be able to learn fairly quickly how much interest and enthusiasm there is for an auction without all of the challenges of a live event.

## C. SILENT AUCTIONS

Silent auctions need a big coordinated effort in order to succeed: First you need to determine when and where the auction will be held. It needs to take place somewhere parents are gathering for something. It makes no sense to have an auction after school one day if no one is going to come. It can be planned around any kind of event –a Halloween carnival, a holiday performance or Spring dance.

The most important thing is getting great items that can be auctioned off. The team of people who are charged with obtaining and acquiring items for any type of auction have their work cut out for them. You can call the team anything you want: procurement, sourcing, or solicitors. I prefer to call it The Get Squad. You can read more about setting up your Get Squad in one of the earlier sections in this book.

Putting together a silent auction is up there with your big dinner party for 12 with the most gourmet, intricate menu you can think of. It's all about the prep: You will want to have a couple of sous chefs help you. You can't have a silent auction without items, and that is what the Get Squad is all about. You need to write letters to past donors as well as new ones, do follow up calls and emails and pickups. You will need to store items until the event too! It's a lot of work and very detail oriented!

Our biggest fundraiser of the school year is usually in May. When I started at the school, I volunteered to co-chair the auction. Our team would take the items that procurement brought in and package them – meaning we would put items together. If we got two tickets to the museum on the other side of town and someone else donated $25 to a restaurant in the same neighborhood, we could combine the items to make a package. This makes the value of the package go up. Then the team wrote up the description for the auction book and finds a place to store all the items. The process started in January, with letters going out to donors.

I realized that we were missing opportunities to get more hotels and restaurants because we started the process so late. If we sent out letters in November, we could get businesses that have budget left for their year-end charitable giving, and/or get on their radar for January. We found that there were a number of hotels that did raffles monthly for organizations like ours and the earlier you submit a request, the better your chances of getting picked.

The items you get should be varied. Think about what YOU would want to bid on and try to get those things. For me, camps and classes are always good, but restaurants and vacations are the items you will make the most money on. It's tough to get hotels to donate if you don't give them enough lead-time. Make life easier on your donors...give them enough time to say YES!

Typically, restaurants will make the most money (getting 90-100% of their value), while health and beauty items bring in 30-40% of their value. Getaways and TV show tapings, such as *Ellen* usually do well, but may not be as easy to come by for your school. It depends on the people in your school community, who they know, and what they do. Everyone can contribute in some way.

The first time you do your auction, you may not be so discriminating about what you get. But after that first auction, take careful consideration about what you want to go after the following year. If you were easily able to get a gift certificate for a $50 facial and it sold for $200, you know you want to get that item again. By contrast, if you put in a lot of effort and time acquiring a dinner and two passes to a movie worth $100 and the item sold for only $25, perhaps you won't work so hard to go after them next year.

You will get items with varying levels of desirability. Some less exciting items may even be donated from people within your school community. You can't do anything about that, but you can redirect where you get outside items. Think about the things you would want for yourself, your kids, your spouse. Set some goals and big-ticket items you would love to be able to get. These are goals. You don't have to share them with anyone. If you get them, GREAT -- If not, don't worry about it.

One mom I spoke with had moved to Pennsylvania from the West Coast and she took most of the fundraising ideas used at her old school to her new one. Here's one of the smartest tips she shared: "Contact other PTO's in other places and trade items that are special in your city, but a rare item in another city. We have lots of Steelers, Pirates, and Penguins Hockey paraphernalia and L.A. had a bunch of mugs and t-shirts from random TV shows and movies. When you trade, the items have more value to the other organization. The grass is always greener..."

When going out to get items, think quality, not quantity. No one will care if you brought in 900 items if no one is interested in half of them. It is better to have quality items that people will want to bid on, rather than a lot of stuff no one wants. The success of your silent auction is dependent on what items you bring to the event.

You need to have organization skills (or work with people who have them) to make sure the event is optimized for the best returns. Think about how you are going to handle the check in/ check out process so that it runs smoothly. Will you have pens with each bid sheet or stickers with last names and bid numbers?

Where you place the tables and where each section will go in the room and how the flow of the room is set up is all very important. If you know that student artwork is always popular, you don't want to stick it in a small corner – it will be uncomfortable and people won't want to stay and bid.

You will need a great team of volunteers. They will help make the event run more smoothly as well as make sure nothing disappears from the auction table before everything has been paid for. Silent auctions take a lot of work but they reap big rewards. Additionally, they can have a galvanizing force in your community and they can be lots of fun. But don't enter into this without your eyes wide open. Silent auctions are big efforts with potentially big rewards.

## SECTION 2: INVOLVING THE KIDS IN THE FUNDRAISING EFFORTS AKA- MEALS WHERE KIDS HELP WITH PREPARATION

Kids like to get involved and feel like they have made a difference. When you cook in the kitchen and give your child a job (no matter how small), they feel a sense of pride when the meal is presented. My daughter beams with pride when our guests arrive and she can tell them she helped to prepare the meal they are eating. The same is true when you're volunteering at the school.

Whether it's having your kids help wash cars at the car wash fundraiser or asking them to put price tags on the items for the all school garage sale, there is a sense of pride that goes along with that task...they know they've helped make a difference. It's a great lesson to teach your kids – whether it's for school or for another organization. Each of us can and should take some ownership and responsibility when it comes to improving or enhancing our community.

## WALK-A-THON

A Walk-a-thon is a great way to teach our kids about healthy habits and philanthropy all at the same time. Kids raise money by walking either per mile or per lap around a track or the schoolyard. Then they get sponsors by asking family and friends for a donation. Some schools ask that you pledge a certain amount (whatever the donor chooses to give) for each lap, while others just ask for a flat donation no matter how many laps the student walks. There are benefits to both. For me, and for many parents I spoke with, they prefer to have students ask for a flat donation. This way they can collect the money up front and not have to wait until after the event to collect money. It is more time efficient for everyone.

The prep work on this includes putting together the forms and making sure every child at the school is aware of the event and wants to participate. You need to get the kids to buy in and this often involves providing incentives for kids who raise the most. You need a lot of hands helping on the big day to assist with water, first aid, getting the kids excited, and keeping spirits high!

Our school walk-a-thon used to raise anywhere from $15-20,000 each year. We held it in the end of November. We sent out information to the kids and collected money up to and after Thanksgiving. It was fine. Solid revenue. The parents who decided to run it this past year, chose to move it to a different time of year. They wanted to try something new.

*Just a side note here about trying something new: You may get resistance from parents who are accustomed to doing things a certain way. You HAVE to try new things. If things are constantly the same, they will be old and boring and tired. Change is good...take it from someone who sometimes has a hard time with it. It can give an annual event a wonderful freshness! Now, back to the Walk-a-thon:*

The people in charge moved the event to February. They scheduled it so it would coincide with the 100th day of school. Their campaign was based on a simple and easy to understand theme: 100 Days, $100. That was the goal. Every child was asked to focus on raising $100 in pledges and sponsorships.

The event chairs covered the campus with posters promoting the event. They knew they wouldn't get $100 from every one of the 900+ students at our school, but they knew they would get *some* of them to give that much. **By providing a clear and straightforward goal, they were able to galvanize support.**

If you're doing a Walk-a-thon, students should send out emails, letters and calls to family members (and family friends!) asking for donations. Then, the student and his or her family is responsible for collecting the payments from their donors. In this way, you make it easier for people to contribute and you share the responsibility for bringing in the money.

At a small private school in Berlin, MD, each of the students were given ten blank address labels with donation letters and were required to mail out the letter requests to friends and families asking for donations. The donations could be as little as $5 and the local bank sponsored the event and donated t-shirts for the participants. The kids walked for 45-minutes and raised $20,000 for their new media lab.

This past year, people at our school were also able to make donations via credit card. This is a huge help to a lot of people. Our school started using an online fundraising tool called Greater Giving. Greater Giving allowed us to take credit card payments for any of our fundraising events. It is just used online; there is not a physical machine to swipe a credit card, but it made it much easier for our community to be able to give – you can donate even while you're in your pajamas at 11:00pm!

The actual event takes some coordination and someone enthusiastic and athletic who runs the day. If you're raising money to support a physical education program, it can be great to have your PE teacher serve as the host.

Here's how the event takes shape: Starting at 9am, each grade comes out to the school's field area. Each grade will spend about 20 minutes walking around the field and trying to walk as many laps as possible in the allotted time. Each classroom's kids dress in a pre-determined color and start at the spot where they see their matching balloons. They have sheets on their backs, and parents mark off a lap each time they go around the track. The music is good and loud. There is a water station with little cups of water for students on the go and students can also bring their own.

At our last Walk-a-thon, students weren't told their parents *had* to give $100. Instead they were encouraged and motivated to get $100 from whatever donors they could solicit (usually grandparents and aunts and uncles and family friends who otherwise might not be able to come to a school event). The kids could go to 10 people and get $10 from each or try to get just $1 from 100 different contributors!

The event coordinators gave incentives to the kids who participated – there was a t-shirt for every child that raised $100 or more and a kindle for the student who raised the most money. This year, they raised $50,000. That is more than double what was raised the year before for the same event!

We raised so much more money primarily because the message and the goals were clearly stated at the beginning of the process. It gave everyone something to shoot for.

If your school isn't doing a Walk-a-thon, perhaps you should consider adding this fundraiser to your core group of events. It is a great way to teach our kids healthy exercise habits that they can use for the rest of their lives while raising money for their school. The students get to have a direct impact on how much money is raised, and it will give them a sense of pride and accomplishment as well.

At a small private preschool in Los Angeles, several families found a unique way to thank donors to their kiddie walk-a-thon. They wrote each donor's name on the event t-shirt and then sent a picture with a thank you note to each donor. This is a nice touch and not necessarily expected. While it may not raise more money, it's a nice way to say thanks, it shows good follow-up, and it sets the stage for another request for support the following year.

## CARNIVAL

A carnival is just what you are imagining it to be. It is a big event that takes place outside with the kids. Maybe it has rides or bounce houses or water slides. Perhaps there are a variety of games and prizes. Maybe there is food. Think hot dogs, burgers and cotton candy instead of gourmet faire – though you could make that work too! It's a fundraiser that is also a "friend-raiser."

You need parents to help organize and get prizes for all the different events, as well as set up of the different booths. This event requires weeks of preparation and a lot of help on the day of. There are a lot of elements to consider so if you choose to take this one on, make sure you have a lot of support!

Our school PTA does a Halloween Carnival every year. Parents buy tickets in $5 bundles or buy a $25 unlimited wristband and kids can play games, go in a haunted shed or even dunk the principal or PTA president if they want. This can be a labor-intensive fundraiser. It requires A LOT of person-power both for the day and in the weeks prior to the big event.

Publicity of the event includes signs and posters all around the campus. Getting the word out to the community through email blasts and room parent messages. Flyers go home in backpacks too! This is a whole school event and it takes a lot of the school to put this event together!

Each classroom has a game or food booth that they are responsible for setting up, volunteering in, and taking down at the end of the day. Parents sign up in the classroom or online to work a shift for 30 minute during the carnival. This can be exhausting for everyone. I know a lot of schools choose to do these as their big fundraiser of the year.

Physically making the booths, prize booths, little kid areas and food areas takes a lot of organization and time. If you have enough volunteers, this can be a great event with lots of community building as well. Once you've held this event for several years, you can usually re-use booths and games year after year so you may only need to make a few new attractions each year.

We know another neighborhood school that sent out flyers to our school to encourage us to come to their carnival. Each flyer included a coupon for 5 game tickets. It brought other schools to the event, helped raise money for the school and again, built stronger ties with the community!

I spoke to a mom at a school in Kansas, who told me their big annual fundraiser is the fall carnival. They sold wristbands for rides and games for $20 per person. Another school in California chose to do their carnival in the Spring and got water slides donated as well. In the years when it is really hot, those booths raised a lot of money.

Being able to create a fun event that is not only fun for your kids, but for lots of people in the community is GREAT! You get to bring people together to have fun and raise money for your school. By having a shared experience like a carnival, everyone is brought closer together and that builds the community to make it stronger.

## BOOK FAIRS AND BOOK EXCHANGE

Book Fairs, whether it's with Scholastic or another company, are good fundraisers that provide kids with the opportunity to buy books and makes some money for the school. Companies usually give a percentage of sales back to your school. They also may give some books to your school library based on your total sales.

These are great events. It's not quite as easy as having a dinner fully catered by a company; it's like having a meal catered and you doing the serving yourself. There is a lot of work involved during the actual book fair, but Scholastic comes in with everything you need and helps with set up. You have to put everything in boxes at the end, but then they come and take it all away again.

The best way to advertise this event is to tag it on to another event that parents want to participate in. A lot of schools try to do their book fairs around the holidays. If there are going to be holiday performances where children will be singing songs, parents will always be there. Because the auditorium may be busy with the holiday shows, the next best place for a book fair might be the school library. This will require you to close the library for two weeks, but it will be worth it for a successful book fair. Teachers should be able to preview the books and make suggestions. Students go through the fair and put things on a wish list. They can then bring those forms home to mom and dad, who will hopefully do some holiday shopping at the book fair after the holiday show performances.

It's always great to get the administration and faculty involved with the book fair. Your Principal and your teachers should have a preview day where they identify their top choices and favorite picks. The Principal's picks and teacher recommendations always end up being top sellers at our school. Teachers also create wish lists and parents will buy for the classroom as well. There are schools that add a philanthropic spin and create wish lists for students at other schools who are less fortunate. Those books get donated to the other school. I like the idea of giving to others when you also give to your own children. It reminds us how lucky we are, and helps remind our kids of that as well.

Because the book fair companies tend to be well-oiled machines, you don't need to do a ton of planning and prep work before the week of the Book Fair. But once the fair is open, you do need some support. As usual, you will need a core group of volunteers. Some will help with crowd control or helping kids find books, and others will help with check out. The volunteers who help with checkout must be trained on the cash register/credit card system and know what they are doing. It gets busy and if you have a flustered volunteer, it could be frustrating for everyone. Sadly, it is also necessary to have volunteers doing security. It's very easy for books to "walk out" during a book fair with lots of kids. You'll want to keep an eye on your "shoppers" to make sure your revenue isn't compromised.

The person in charge of this event will be in constant contact with the book fair company. Whether it's Scholastic or another independent company, you will need to be able to restock popular books and the impulse buy knick-knacks at the register. It's important to get the reorders in by the deadline, so that you aren't without items the next day.

Depending on what company you partner with for a book fair, there may be different ways your school can receive compensation. You may be able to get money; you may also be able to get credits toward book or library furniture purchases from that company's catalogue. It is best to know ahead of time how you will want to take your profits. If, for example, you earned $500 from the sales, the company will give you a choice of taking the $500 OR getting $800 worth of stuff from their catalogue. Make sure you take the time to figure out what's best for your school. You can get more dollar value, but if you're school needs cash, you should take that and use it.

*Offsite Book Fairs*: If you cannot do a book fair at your school, you can do an offsite book fair with Barnes & Noble. They can host book fairs at their brick and mortar stores and online. If there's no Barnes & Noble nearby, you might also be able to partner with a local bookstore if they are willing to do it.

You'll want to work with your local bookstore to encourage parents and kids to come in to the store. Work with them to try to create events during the weekend that all the families will want to attend. Maybe they have someone reading stories, or a book signing, or some special event. Ask teachers to provide recommended book lists so you can have them available at the store for the event. If you get people interested in attending, they will show up and more importantly, they will BUY. The percentage the school gets online will be smaller than at the physical store, so anything you can do to get bodies into the store and spread the word is a good thing.

*Used Books/ Book Exchange*: A mom in Tennessee told me about this simple fundraiser that encourages reading and sharing of great books. Her kids go to a private K-12 school called University School of Nashville. They do several fundraisers throughout the year (in addition to their Annual Fund Drive). One fundraiser is a used book sale. "Everyone donates books, both kid and adult books and they sell them to the public for $1-2 each. It makes a mint and you can rid yourself of all your junk!" This could be set up at a local Farmer's Market or as a Garage Sale in your driveway!

In conclusion, any fundraiser that encourages reading serves a dual purpose – it raises money while also encouraging good educational habits. Therefore book-based fundraisers are easily promotable as being central to your school's educational mission- preferable to candy bars, which don't necessarily support an educational priority.


## PERSONALIZED NOTE CARDS AND MORE...

What parent doesn't think their son or daughter is the next Picasso, Matisse, or Thomas Kinkade? Notecards and other products featuring student's original artwork are always a popular fundraising program. These are popular in pre schools and elementary schools alike. There's nothing better than giving grandma a set of notecards with artwork created by the grandkids! There are companies like www.printartkids.com that work directly with art teachers and/or the PTA to take your children's artwork and turn it into note cards or plates or anything else that grandparents would love and use.

This fundraiser can be very time consuming for the one or two people running it. It is important to get all the teachers involved and have them plan for students to create individual pieces of art that can be used for these types of projects. Your program coordinators or the teachers can assign a different theme per class or grade. Students do the artwork, and parents sign a release stating that it's ok to take their child's work and turn it into something they might buy.

It takes some effort to organize each class and keep all the paperwork and order forms together to send off to the company. Once that's done, your coordinator is finished until it's time to distribute the orders. When the delivery day arrives, it is always fun for the kids to see how their artwork has been transformed.

A public school in Montana ran with this idea and created an exciting program highlighting the school's commitment to art and creativity. "The Original Projects" became a school-wide event.

One of the teachers worked with the PTA to spread the word. Every class in the school did a separate activity specifically for Original Works and the classroom teachers worked with the PTA liaison to ensure that everyone was included. Each child brought home an order form that was just like a picture form with the child's artwork showcased on oven mitts, key chains, coffee mugs...anything you can imagine.

Parents ordered what they wanted and turned the forms in to their child's teacher. The teacher then gave it to the PTA liaison and the PTA president and the teacher worked on delivering items and dealing with the money.

A portion of all sales goes directly to the school. This is a great fundraiser in schools that want to highlight their commitment to the arts. Everyone wants to be able to have an art keepsake of their child's work...and to be able to share it with every member of the family!

## CLASS ART PROJECTS

Unlike the previous fundraiser, this one focuses on group projects. It may take some coordination and creativity on the part of parents in each classroom, but the result can mean big bucks for the school.

Imagine having each student working on part of a big art project that can later be auctioned off at a school auction or art show. Group projects will get parents bidding against each other for that one-of-a-kind piece. You can create anything from a painted table and chair set, a photo album of the students' favorite thing about the school (pictures taken by the kids of course), or a painted lemonade pitcher and glasses. If the kids make it, the parents want to buy it! An end of semester art show can be a wonderful culminating event and can also serve as a fundraiser for the school.

## FREE DRESS DAYS

Looking for a simple, no effort fundraiser? This is as close to a TV dinner as you can get! At a private school in Hawaii, students wear uniforms every day. One of the fundraisers they do is a simple free dress day. The kids give $1 and bring in a can when they have free dress days. The $1 goes to a fund and the can goes to the Maui Food Bank. The money raised goes to the school and they are teaching the kids about giving to others. When we can instill this in our children at a young age, they will always think about how they can make a difference in someone else's life.

Getting children involved in a fundraising or philanthropic endeavor provides a great educational opportunity. When we show our kids how they can be a big part of helping their school raise money, we not only help the school, we teach our children a valuable lesson about the importance of education, giving back and helping others.

## SECTION 3: COMMUNITY EVENTS- BUILDING COMMUNITY AND GENERATING REVENUE AKA THE POT LUCK...

Having a big dinner party can be lovely, but isn't it also fun to have a big community potluck where everyone can contribute and bring something special to the festivities? The fundraisers listed in this section are similar to a potluck. There are a lot of people involved in helping and everyone gets to share in the responsibility.

## ICE CREAM, PIZZA, POPCORN, & BAKE SALES

At our school, the $5^{th}$ grade students and teachers sell ice cream to raise money for their culmination party, graduation, and the $5^{th}$ grade overnight trip. One of the $5^{th}$ grade teachers buys the ice cream wholesale and gets reimbursed from the booster club's $5^{th}$ grade account. The teacher sets up a schedule for the year in four-week blocks and every day after school, the ice cream shop is open for business. There are always two teachers and four students selling. The teachers train students to sell items, though most of the time it's on-the-job training. This is great for the students because it teaches them a sense of responsibility, how to work as a team, and what it's like to have a job.

"It's a rite of passage," said the teacher I spoke with. They learn about restocking items when they get low, keeping the ones that melt fast in the freezer (so they don't lose money on it), and how to make change. They are rewarded with an ice cream at the end of the week for their service. Ice cream sales grossed just over $20,000 last year – that doesn't take into account the cost for the ice cream, but even if it netted half of that, $10,000 is nothing to sneeze at.

Fifth grade also sells pizza and popcorn at other events like Open House, Back to School Night, Movie Night, Music Night, Halloween Carnival and any other happenings on campus where parents and students congregate. Parents take the lead on organizing these sales. There is a parent with a pizza place who gives the school a discount -- $5 for a large cheese and $6 for a large pepperoni and the kids sell them for $2/slice. There are 10 slices in each and they profit $15 for each cheese pizza and $14 for each pepperoni pizza. Parents handle the money and give it to the 5th grade chairperson for the booster club so the money can be deposited into the bank. The best way to make money on drinks is to ask parents to donate flats of water or soda – then it's pure profit!

There is real potential for A LOT of money from these sales. It will take A LOT of coordination and A LOT of volunteers to keep it up throughout the year. But it also helps to create a stronger community, as everyone loves hanging out after school by the ice cream. This is not an easy undertaking, by any means, but it may be worth the work for a 5th grade fundraiser or for the school.

## GOLF TOURNAMENT

There are several schools I spoke with that host an annual golf tournament to raise money. Golf tournaments are a great way to get dads involved in an event (not that moms don't golf – but there are generally more men participating). Some schools charge a per golfer fee, while others charge per group of four. I spoke with a dad who organized a lot of tournaments in Texas, before moving to California. To create an event like a golf tournament, you must start a year in advance. You need to get major sponsors: the golf course, the beer or beverage sponsor, and a "hole in one" car sponsor. It will take at least 6 months to a year to do all that because corporations need to plan for these types of donations as part of their annual budget for major gifts. If you think this might be an annual event, you should let them know in advance. Once you've got organizations signed on, it's relatively easy to get them to come back and support the cause year after year.

Your school should try to get the golf course to allow you to hold your tournament at a reduced fee. Some might suggest holding the event on an off day while others negotiate lower fees during the low season. Your biggest challenge will be finding sponsors to donate food and drinks. I talked to one parent who was able to get the local BMW dealership to agree to give a car to anyone who got a hole in one. This was great advertising for the dealership. In three years of involvement, they have yet to give a car away.

Once you've identified your venue and major sponsors, you have to focus on recruiting golfers and donations for a small silent auction (see the section on silent auctions to learn more about how to do this). The best way to attract participants is with a simple brochure. At the school I spoke with, they formed a committee of 10-15 people who secured donations for the auction and found golfers. This team was part Get Squad and part marketing team. It's important to have a strong team as there is a lot of legwork required.

The event can be set up in a variety of different ways but generally the golfing takes place throughout the day and then there is a dinner and silent auction in the evening. If you have dads who like to golf, this can be a great new way to get them involved and it will help diversify your fundraising while broadening the community you're serving with your events.

Depending on the cost of golfing in your area, the entry fee for your tournament may vary. Here in California, they had no difficulty getting golfers to pay $700 per team of 4 (that's $175 each). The fee includes golfing, greens fees, the golf cart and dinner. Additionally, companies can sponsor a team of golfers and that's another great source of revenue for your school fundraising.

The economics are fairly straightforward. The school had to pay $85 per golfer for the event and $40 per guest for the dinner. So for every golfer who paid $175, they made $50 in profit. For guests who only wanted to come to the dinner, they charged $50 per person so they added an additional $10 per guest in profit for the dinner portion of the event.

To increase the money they made, they added a small silent auction. They also had a grand prize raffle of a trip to Arizona. There were door prizes of gift certificates. They also added to the event by awarding trophies for 1st, 2nd and 3rd place as well as for the lowest scoring team. They also gave recognition prizes for "longest drive" for men or women and "closest to the pin" (on a par 3) was awarded a set of golf balls.

If you have golfers in your community, a golf tournament can be a wonderful way to spend a day, can broaden the sources of support your school looks to, and can generate a lot of good will in the community. And if you are able to find ways to make the event even more engaging, with awards, and a silent auction, and a raffle and door prizes, you're likely to create something truly memorable and very lucrative for your school.

## BINGO NIGHTS

A lot of towns across the United States have Bingo Nights. Usually it's associated with a church or temple. But there are game nights popping up in big cities too, and there's no reason not to take advantage of a good night out and make money for your school at the same time!

There is a Catholic private school in Virginia that has done just that! The men's club from the church runs the weekly Bingo game, and the school is required to provide 16 volunteer parents each week. This school had enough parents that the commitment meant each parent needed to volunteer just two times. (this is a very small commitment but for those parents who couldn't do it, they had the option to donate $200 to opt out).

The men's club donates the net proceeds to the school, a very healthy chunk of change! The school was able to get a gaming license because they are affiliated with the church, which already had the license and was doing the weekly Bingo game. The school needed more money than the church, so the school got the money.

This same school also sold raffle tickets from the middle of September through October and the drawings started November 1. The low prizes were crafty home made knick-knacks and $100 gift cards and the high prize was $1,000. The raffle brought in about $70,000 – much more than expected.  The child who sold the most raffle tickets won an iPad.

## HOLIDAY BOUTIQUE

Everyone needs to buy gifts at the holidays for family, friends, and teachers!  Why not create an opportunity for families to shop and give back to the school?  Also, if you have parents who do craft-type businesses, you can invite them to sell their merchandise. It gets them some new customers while also bringing revenue into the school.

Think about how big you want this event to be.  Are you willing to rent tables and chairs? tablecloths?  Will it be a one day event or over the course of a few days?  Do vendors have to participate in all the days?  How will you advertise the event?  Is there something else happening at the school at the same time to bring people in?  Are you doing it on a weekend? After school?  At night?  Is it an outdoor event?  Is there a plan if it rains?  It's very important to find just the right time and place for this event to make it work well.

Advertising is key.  A lot of temples and churches do these events as well.  Sometimes they do it over the course of a few days and charge more for the table fees. These groups tend to schedule their events so that the boutique is open for business before or after their weekly religious services. In this way, they are able to guarantee that at least some people will attend.

The hardest part of doing an event like this is getting the parents to come. Marketing is a big piece of this.  If there is something there that can draw people in, it helps.   One public school I spoke with does a BOO-tique.   They incorporate the craft boutique into their Halloween carnival so they know they will have a bunch of people coming. The Boo-tique is an add-on that keeps people staying at the event longer and hopefully spending more money.

Many organizations that host these boutiques charge vendors a fee to display their stuff – basically a table fee, plus a percentage (varies from 10-20%) of what they make that day.

There are two different ways of setting up payment at the boutique. The first is to have the vendors take their own payments and give a percentage back to you at the end of the event. This can be good if you know and trust all the vendors and don't have too many to keep track of. The more common practice is to have one central pay station that someone on your team is in charge of. You either provide or ask the vendors to provide receipt books in triplicate so that the person buying takes two to the cashier and brings one back stamped "paid." The vendor keeps that receipt and the customer gets one with their item. Each receipt must have the vendor's booth number or name so they can get credit for the sale.

If you choose to run the event with a central cashier, you will need to write checks to each vendor and get them out within a few weeks after the event. This is time consuming and requires good organization skills.

Holiday Boutiques are a great way to support local artisans and expose your community to great items while also supporting your school.

## COOKBOOK FUNDRAISERS

Similar to the previous fundraiser, cookbook fundraisers require organization to assemble all the pieces of the pie! In one effort in Western Massachusetts, the parents created a cookbook for grades K-2. The parents used a website called Lulu.com. One mom laid the book out in Microsoft Word and did the cover in Photoshop. You need to upload a PDF to Lulu, though, so you could do the layout in any program and then make a PDF.

The mom I spoke with told me that "this is definitely doing it the hard way, and you need someone who can do a layout and knows at least a little bit about publishing - but you get a much more customized book. You can also go through one of the fundraising cookbook companies - it's less work, but the trade-off is a plastic spiral binding, which I would do pretty much anything to avoid!"

They ordered 300 copies on Lulu and because it was a large order, they only had to pay $5.38 each for them (including shipping). They sold their customized cookbooks for $15/each. This means they were able to make just under $10 for each cookbook they sold. If they had bought the cookbooks individually from Lulu, they'd be about $9 each. Ordering a large initial number of cookbooks enabled them to get a significant discount.

When I last checked in with the school, they had sold a little over 200 copies. Generally when you do a cookbook or any book featuring student or family contributions, you should order 3 books per family that participates. They had 105 families contribute so their initial order was 300 books. They're not worried that they won't be able to sell the rest of the books. They'll be selling them at the Farmer's Market and Ashland Day and whenever there is a community event.

Cookbook Fundraisers are a great way to build community. When you share recipes and stories, you get to know your fellow parents in a new way. The cookbook may lead to an invitation to dinner if someone really likes your recipe. It may create opportunities for sharing family stories and engaging with other parents on a whole new level. You know I like to cook. And for those of us who love cooking, we're learning new things while benefitting the school. Now that's a recipe for success!

## COMMUNITY GARAGE SALE

A school in New York had great success doing a community garage sale. Each family that wanted to participate rented space in the school parking lot and gave a percentage of their sales to the school. If you plan it out, this event can bring in a lot of money for the school. Remember- one family's trash may be another family's treasure. Make arrangements with The Salvation Army or another nonprofit to pick up the excess at the end of the day.

# CAR WASH

Doing a car wash can be a fun way to get kids and adults involved in raising some cash for the school. Pick a weekend date that should be warm. Give yourselves plenty of time to organize and advertise. The parent I spoke to had theirs from 12noon to 4pm - each 5th grade classroom covered one hour. The one-hour shifts worked well for them. The dad I spoke to suggested keeping in contact with the room parents to make sure they have enough volunteers. You will need lots of people!

Find a place to do it – preferably in a high-traffic area so people can find you. A local church agreed to let the school hold the event on their upper parking lot. Because the event was in the parking lot, the parents did not need to worry about getting insurance.The organizers gave the church a small donation ($100) for the water and power after the event.

Then you need to get the word out. Make signs and put them up. Let everyone in the community know about it. The school charged $6 for tickets purchased before the event and $8 the day of event. ($2 more for larger cars, trucks and vans). They sold tickets when they sold popcorn and ice cream, at carpool pick up, and at Open House.

On the day of the event, you will need three long hoses, four heavy duty extension cords, three shop vacuums (to clean the inside), eight large buckets, lots of BIG sponges, soap, LOTS of towels, and a cash box so you can make change. Have each class bring their own soap, towels and sponges and a happy attitude!

There is something really fun about having your friends wash your car. The kids love it. They put on their bathing suits and have a blast! They also set up some tables to sell water, chips and cookies. Some of the girls also sold some duct tape items they made (they donated $75 from their sales to the school).

One of the dads who was really involved commented, "If there was one event that brought our entire 5th grade together, this was it. The kids, teachers and parents from all four classes really bonded. Lots of wet children went home in very clean cars, and our principal was a huge supporter of this event. He helped clean cars for hours!" After the donation to the church, the event raised $1,600.

## INTERNATIONAL NIGHT- A REAL OLD FASHIONED POT LUCK

A Texas elementary school with about 650 students hosted an International night. The mom I spoke with told me that parents made and served authentic food from various countries and raised a bunch of money.

The parents of each country wore the clothing of their country and served the food. Mexico was represented by nachos and burritos, Asian parents served eggrolls and fried rice, and the Native Americans sold delicious Indian Fried Bread. The other parents sold drinks, popcorn and hot dogs.

Each booth was decorated in native décor. Everyone had a great time and the kids got to experience a little taste of other cultures and taste the food of the various countries. This was an event that took place after school (4-6pm) and the total amount raised was $3800.

This could have a real fair-like feel to the event. There is a lot of work to put in, and advertising to get a big crowd. But in communities where cultural diversity and tolerance of other cultures is a key educational goal for the school, this kind of activity can be very meaningful for the neighborhood. And as long as it is raising money for the school, why not give it a try!

## SECTION 4: INVOLVING NEIGHBORHOOD BUSINESSES AKA ORDERING TAKE OUT

If it hasn't been made clear just how important the businesses around your school are to your school, let me make sure you know: THEY ARE CRUCIAL!! You need to engage the whole community. The strongest schools benefit from strong ties to their local business communities. It is also important for the children to have a first-hand experience of civic engagement. When the school thrives, businesses thrive and home values go up. Businesses get more business when they support the local school and parents find new, exciting places to go in the neighborhood to spend money! It's a win-win for everyone!

## RESTAURANT NIGHTS

A lot of school groups take advantage of the community around them. They work with local restaurants, ice cream shops, and juice bars to do special days that will support their schools or sports teams. Some schools do these monthly, with a different restaurant each month. Others do them just a few times a year. It's good for the school and it's good for the local business. Typically, the restaurant draws in a lot of new business and then gives a percentage (10-25%) back to the school.

All restaurants are not the same, so make sure you check with the management/owners to get the best rate you can. The best I've ever seen has been 25% of sales. Sometimes they want customers to bring in a special coupon, others will take 25% of all sales.

If you do try to get a restaurant to participate in a Restaurant Night, call and speak with the owner or manager, and follow up in person, rather than email. Restaurateurs are community-minded and focused on one-on-one in person interactions. It's the basis of their business. It's always best to meet them on their terms and on their turf.

California Pizza Kitchen was a standard option for our school. We used to hold monthly restaurant nights there and they would give back a percentage of sales. Then our school started branching out and choosing a few other restaurants in the neighborhood. CPK wasn't as happy, but the other local restaurants were thrilled with the response from the parents and they gave up to 25% back to the school.

The prep work on this is minimal. Not a lot of work, and a whole lot of payoff! You need to get the restaurants to commit, but they will want to be involved because it brings in business! You publicize the event, and encourage parents to go. In some cases, you'll have to make the flyer that parents have to present at the restaurant and then get it distributed within your community.

Some places like Jamba Juice, Coffee Bean & Tea Leaf, or Pinkberry will also come to your school events and give a percentage of the revenue to the school. Having these businesses at an all school picnic, kinder picnic, Back-to-School Night or Open House is always good business for them, and easy money for the school.

## PANCAKE BREAKFAST/ HOLIDAY PARTY

There's another restaurant fundraiser that can provide a big boost to your fundraising efforts: A restaurant donates food and drink for a party on a specific day during a two or three hour period when they are normally closed. Parents pay a certain amount to attend. All money raised goes to the school and the restaurant takes the tax deduction. This can be a brunch or an early dinner. It can be with kids or without – depending on what your school community wants to do and what the restaurant is willing to donate.

A mom in Park City, Utah, told me about a fundraiser she did for the school orchestra. "They needed to raise money to travel to a competition so they did a dinner fundraiser in a local restaurant. We offered a set menu – with so much of each ticket going to the orchestra. We also raffled off donated prizes. The orchestra entertained the parents throughout the evening. It was quite fun - kids sold dinner and raffle tickets beforehand. They raised quite a lot of money."

Here's what another school does – this time, involving the kids as waiters and waitresses! A major restaurant (that doesn't usually do breakfast) opens up and donates food and let's the kids partake in setting up, helping with service (as best they can, it's the elementary school) and the parents get tickets to sell to the community for $10 or $20.

The advertising on this is not just school-wide, but community-wide. The local paper puts in stories about the event and advertises it (which helps promote the local restaurant as well). The kids feel like they are a huge part of the event and have made a difference for their school.

## RAFFLES

Raffles come in all shapes and sizes. Some schools do raffles every day for a month to up your chances of winning items, while others do just a few items and tie it into a bigger event. Some parents buy items to be raffled off, while others go out to the community and ask for donations. All of these raffles are good. The most important thing is getting something that people will want to get.

In Montana, a local car dealer donated a Toyota Scion and they sold raffle tickets for it. The dealer was a parent at the school and for him, it was a good tax write off, and a great way to raise money for the school. Another school in Los Angeles was able to get the local Vespa store to donate a Vespa at a discounted price. The school had to pay half the cost of the retail price of the Vespa and then they sold raffle tickets. The people in charge reimbursed the booster club fund for the initial cost of the Vespa, and any money they made over that, was profit from the raffle. The Vespa raffle didn't make a ton of money – certainly not what a car would bring in, but the cost to do a car raffle was pricey ($250/ticket) and the winner had to pay for tax and license too.

In a small private Catholic school in Virginia, the kids do a Super Raffle. Each family is responsible for selling 10 tickets (700) kids. Tickets are $10 each so each family is responsible for selling $100 in tickets. Then every weekday during the month of November, they draw a ticket for a predetermined amount of money ($100-$1,000) that goes to the lucky winner. They cleared approximately $70,000 last year.

Similarly, at one school in Rhode Island, the students sell raffle tickets every October for $10 each. Each child's goal is to sell 10 of them. They give away cash/prizes every day during October - some items are donated, some come from the money they raise. Items range from a $10 Jamba Juice gift card to a $50 gift card to a restaurant or movie theatre. They do very well with it. Parents and students prefer it to a million different candle/cookie dough fundraisers all year.

Raffles are a great way to make money. If you live in a city with tickets to sporting events and concerts, theatre experiences or television tapings, you can find a way to raffle them off. Sometimes banks are willing to offer a cash prize for raffles. If you can get a cash prize, do it. Cash prize raffles tend to attract the most interest and generate the best raffle ticket sales.

My daughter's swim team was able to get an iPad from Best Buy and raffle that off. Sometimes companies will donate items and other times, parents will offer to pay for a big ticket item to raffle off; getting the word out about the raffle takes time, but the payoff is usually worth it!

## CAR DEALERSHIP PARTNERSHIP

The prep work on this has more to do with building the relationship. I personally have tried for YEARS to get a car to raffle off, but I have not been so lucky! Sometimes it takes years to cultivate a relationship with a company to get them to commit. Other times, you get lucky and one of your parents owns a dealership and is willing to help. Even if you can't convince someone to donate a car for a raffle, you might be able to get something. Remember: you have to ask!

I spoke with a parent who said that one of the parents at their school owns a car dealership, They didn't donate a car, but they did have a weekend where for every test-drive they did, the dealership would donate a set amount to the school. They brought the cars to a neighborhood parking lot and set up test-drives there. For every test drive that a parent took, the school would get $25 or $50.  For many parents, they simply participated so they could generate a donation for the school. But if anyone was seriously looking at buying a new car, the dealership had a better chance of making a sale, and the school benefitted.  This isn't going to be a huge money-maker, but it's definitely worth considering.

## FAMILY PHOTOS FOR THE HOLIDAYS

At a private school in Tennessee, the lower school Photo Project has happened each Spring. The photographer, who is also a parent at the school comes to school and takes black and white photos of each student - one class at a time. The room parents alert their classes to the days/time of their kids' session. Parents volunteer to comb kids' hair & wipe their noses before each child steps in front of the camera. Nobody is out of the classroom for more than 20 minutes.

A few weeks later, the photos go up in the long hallway of the school and parents can come and buy the 4x6.  They have a reception with cookies and coffee where parents can review the photos of their beautiful children. They also leave them up for a week for parents who are unable to make it to the event.  If a parent wants a picture, they buy it for $35. One year, the photographer offered discs with all the photos from the session for $55.  The money for the 4x6 prints and for the discs went to the school, but if parents wanted larger prints or color prints or extra copies they would pay the photographer.

I asked this mom if the parents ever feel like this shows favoritism to that one photographer.  I know at our school there are plenty of great photographers, and it would be uncomfortable to ask one over another to donate this event (and let them make some money off of it as well).  The mom told me that the photographer has been doing it since her daughter started at the school, and she will likely continue until she graduates. This is wonderful.  If there is a parent who is willing to give their time to help coordinate this kind of fundraiser, I think you should do it. Not all school communities are so open to it, but if yours is, I think you should try it.

## SCENTSY

I spoke with a mom in Washington who sells candles and fragrances as a Scentsy consultant. One of her fellow Scentsy reps did a fundraiser with one of the local elementary schools. Every student brought home the Scentsy catalogue and took orders from friends and family. They were given a certain amount of time to collect orders and money. The Scentsy rep donated her commission to the school. At the school event, she sold about $4000 in product and she gave the school 30% back.

There are other companies that have reps (maybe even at your school) who would be willing to do a fundraiser and give back. You never know unless you ask!

## SECTION 5: PASSIVE INCOME: RAISING MONEY WITH LESS EFFORT AKA SOMETIMES A MICROWAVE DINNER DOES THE TRICK

It's always great when you can raise money for your school and it doesn't take any time away from what you'd normally do in your day. Sometimes you want the frozen Stouffer's dinner – you don't want to take the time to make a big steak dinner – especially when the frozen Salisbury steak takes just minutes to heat up. Right? The same holds true for these fundraising ideas. You may be doing this stuff anyway – shopping online, going to the market, etc. Why not help your school make some money at the same time.

## ESCRIP AND OTHER ONLINE SHOPPING

School districts throughout the country are using online shopping to boost their fundraising. Big schools, small schools, independent and public as well as a lot of sports teams are tapping into the web to make a few extra dollars. While many still use escrip, others are finding that affiliate programs such as *Click. Buy. Help.,* Schoola, and Paperless PTO are bringing in much-needed money just by having parents and friends shop online as they would normally.

These companies take a small percentage of each sale. Parents need to go to the school's web page and click on the link to the particular store they want to shop at. Then with every purchase, the school gets a percentage of the sale. The percentage is dependent on the store. It can range anywhere from 3% to 25%. Schools that have used these services have reported that they get their money promptly and it is less of a hassle than escrip. Still, there are schools that are devoted to escrip and love it.

## THE TARGET RED CARD AND
## OTHER BRANDED SHOPPING CARDS

Target also gives back if you use their credit card. You can designate your school on your Target RedCard and they will donate 1% of your purchase back to your school. You will also get a 5% discount on your purchases.

Vons and Ralphs supermarkets set up a program to give back to the school of your choice with every swipe of your rewards card, based on certain purchases. Other supermarkets across the country do this as well. You need to renew them every year, but the money does add up.

Office Depot and Staples have similar reward programs that give back to schools as well. Every purchase helps, and if you're buying this stuff anyway, why not help the school at the same time?

# SECTION 6: SELLING STUFF AKA THE LEMONADE STAND

## SPIRIT STORE

A great way to build excitement in your school community and raise some money as well is by setting up a spirit store. You can sell items such as hats, t-shirts, sweatshirts, jackets, pencils, flashlights and blankets and luggage tags for kids and adults with the school name on it.

It's hard to know what will sell. In order to not get stuck with a lot of shirts that no one wants, one school created an order form and printed only what was purchased. This can be good, but a lot of people miss out on the excitement of purchasing and walking away with the item. You could also do limited supply of items and see what is a big seller. This will change every year, so you have to just try and take some risks.

## GIFT WRAP, CANDY, AND MORE...

At a school in Georgetown, TX, a mom of 3 boys tells me that fundraising was a big topic for their elementary school. They have about 500 plus students, and have always done fundraisers where they are reselling products from a partner store. They sell some kind of item- gift wrap, candles, etc. and a percentage goes back to the school. In the past, they've been able to get as much as 50% of the sales donated back to the school. Everything is dependent on the company you work with as well as how much you sell.

They have also done short giving campaigns where they will take two weeks and ask for money from the school community and friends and family. For the past two years they have had great success from these events -- giving incentives for kids to turn in money over a two or three week period. Classrooms that raised the most money received a popsicle party. 100% of the money raised goes to the school.

The key to the program's success was having a clear and well-established goal for how much they'd make as well as a plan for what the money would fund. Once again, it's all about communicating with the families.

At a school in Colorado, one of the Parent-Teacher Organizations does fundraising through a company called ABC fundraising. Parents order stuff like wrapping paper and various random things and they make it a class competition. The winning class gets a pizza party and the winning teacher gets a Barnes & Noble gift card. This event makes about $20,000 for the school each year. The Principal gets involved to motivate student participation. On one occasion, he offered to shave his head if the fundraising reached a certain goal. This mom told me that "the kids love it because he follows through! One year he sat on stage in their cafeteria in a baby pool and pretended he was a human sundae. The kids squirted ice cream toppings on him as they all came through for lunch."

I spoke with a mom in Florida who told me that her daughter's public elementary school did the Otis Spunkmeyer cookie sales for a fundraiser. "I always end up buying $100 worth of cookies and you should SEE all the cases of cookies in the cafeteria on pick up day!! All the other selling fundraisers, I poop out on – and I just write a check."

Coupon books are also a BIG seller. A parent I spoke with sells the Save Around books and makes 50% profit and brings in about $7,000 (selling in September). Entertainment Books also have a similar program where you can buy the books for $30 and up to 50% will go back to the school.

Entertainment Books has also branched out so they can help you fundraise not just with the books. They can also provide gourmet cookie dough and gift wrap through a partner company, Sally Foster. Sally Foster sends items directly to the buyers so you don't have to organize and deliver to classrooms. They give 40% back to the school, while Innisbrook, which also does gift wrap, cookies, chocolate and school supplies donates 50% of gift wrap sales and 45% of all other sales back to the school.

A mom in Washington State told me that her schools

have always done Payback books. Payback Books follow the model of Entertainment Books but they are more geographically targeted with coupons for local businesses. They sell the books for $20 and the school gets to keep 50% of the sales price.

There are other companies that sell reusable bags. This is a very popular one in Southern California since we are trying to get rid of the plastic bag option at the supermarket. There are many sizes and design choices and they also give a percentage back to the school.

Some other online fundraising companies are below. I'm not endorsing any of these, and I haven't had any personal experience with them. Parents all over the country who have used them and like them have shared them with me. This is why I wanted to share them with you.

http://www.thirtyonegifts.com/ -This company has totes and purses, and carriers to help you transport food and drinks to a party, as well as other organizational items.

http://flowerpowerfundraising.com -Flower Power has a face-to-face catalog fundraising program. Their program features direct shipments to customers, a 100% money-back guarantee, a quality pledge, and a 50% profit margin.

http://www.ezfund.com -They have easy fundraising ideas with quality products and services. They provide products with full support to make your fundraiser successful! Some items include Smencils, candy, flowers, gourmet treats, candles, and lollipops.

http://www.originalworks.com -Original Works transforms each child's artwork onto individual, quality products that could be shared with family and friends.

## INCOME FROM RECYCLING

At a school in Hawaii, the 5th grade collects recyclables year round for their trip to Oahu. They stand at the pick up/drop off lines daily with signs reminding parents and fellow students to bring in cans etc. On pre-determined days once a month, a parent volunteer stays at the recycle center near the school so members of the community can drop their recyclables with her. The school uses all the cash back from recycling for their trip.

## SECTION 7: THINKING BIGGER: OTHER CALIFORNIA DISTRICTS, OTHER WAYS AKA THROW A COMMUNITY PICNIC

I have met people in the Santa Monica/Malibu School District as well as Las Virgenes School District who have started doing centralized fundraising for their districts. Because they have fewer schools in their district, they raise money for all the schools in the area and split the amount raised equally among the schools.

For the past 18 years, the non-profit organization, Manhattan Beach Education Foundation, has been hosting a wine auction to raise money for the seven schools in Manhattan Beach. They provide grants to the seven public schools in their district. The local country club hosts the event (so no one pays for the use of the space) – which is the largest charity wine auction in Southern California. It features food, wine, live music and dancing, and live and silent auctions. It sells out with 1400 guests each year.

The Las Virgenes school district is following suit. T.H.E. Foundation is the non-profit that raises money for their school district. Their sole purpose is to narrow the widening gap between funds required to maintain the excellence of the schools and those that the state provides. This year their first annual fundraiser, T.H.E. Event, grossed over $400,000 with just over 1,000 guests! Of that, they gave $200,000 to the schools in the district, and put aside more for later disbursement.

The Santa Monica-Malibu Unified School District has recently adopted this centralized fundraising policy. School PTAs used to raise money and spend money for their own school. Now it goes in one pot for all schools to be divided. Schools can no longer raise money to hire personnel and to support programs and services eliminated because of SMMUSD budget cuts. The nonprofit Santa Monica-Malibu Education Foundation is now in charge of these efforts. As a result, some parents are giving less money to the fundraising. One parent that I spoke with told me her daughter's school is completely cutting the arts programs for K thru 2. She is hopeful, however, that this new system will be more equitable for everyone. She said, "People need to do the right thing for ALL the kids, not just their own." The difference between the other two school districts noted here and SMMUSD is that the other two are fairly affluent school districts, while Santa Monica-Malibu has both wealthy and middle class families who live within the district.

Businesses that are on the 3rd Street Promenade (Santa Monica's upscale outdoor mall close to the beach) have an additional tax put on them to help with the schools as well. It's a high cost to the business owner, but people shopping in the area are primarily tourists, and the businesses are making a decent amount of money from them.

I spoke with a mom in Texas who gave in an unusual way. "I have supported the school in a very specific way for the past two years. I teach at UT (University of Texas) and have a donor who gives money to support training and research into the impact of arts in education on the campus. I started this before I decided to send my daughter to the school. I've spent 2 1/2 years training all the teachers on the campus on how to use drama-based instruction to teach across the curriculum. I also raise money at UT to send teachers to our professional development programs in the summer that I run at the University. So I've raised over $40,000 in services for the school to provide training and support for teachers. It's a unique idea, which probably won't work for many other folks as it reflects my unique position as a University professor who also runs training for K-12 schools and the fact that I have access to donors and research dollars is unusual."

# A FEW LAST WORDS

Raising money for your children's school is a big responsibility. It isn't something that you can do alone. You must be able to work within a group. You need the support of the administration, teachers, business community and fellow parents. Not everyone will get on board this fundraising train. It's important to share the responsibility and not take control of every little piece of it.

One of the most important parts of raising money is sharing the information with the rest of the parent body. If your booster club is representing the best interests of the students (and parents), you must keep them informed and let them have a say about how the money is spent. Communication is key to the success of any fundraising effort.

One school I researched sends a one sheet home and posts it on the school website letting everyone know where the money that was raised was spent. Other schools do surveys asking parents how they think the money should be spent. Transparency is important. If the parents don't trust the people running the booster club to make decisions that mirror their values, it can be difficult to get anything done.

Creating a way for people to provide feedback allows everyone an opportunity to learn from one another. I'd love to hear your feedback about this book. I'm also eager to hear any stories you'd like to share about your school fundraising experiences. We're all in this together and we all want to find ways to improve our school's efforts. Most importantly, we can learn from each others' experiences.

Please make a point to stop by our website, A Mom's Guide To Fundraising (www.amomsguidetoschoolfundraising.com) or visit us at our Facebook page: https://www.facebook.com/AMomsGuideToFundraising. While you're there, please "Like" the page! If social media isn't your thing, feel free to send an email to me at sbmomsguide@gmail.com. But please- do reach out to me. I am genuinely interested in your feedback, your stories, and building a strong and supportive community.

As you have no doubt figured out, fundraising can be challenging. But given what's at stake, the future of our children, I think you'll agree that it's worth the effort. It's impossible to please everyone 100% of the time. But if you can make an impact on the lives of children in your community, any effort is worthwhile. Just remember to do your best...always...and keep putting the kids first when making decisions about where to spend the money.

## ABOUT THE AUTHOR

Sarah Barrett has a Masters in Education from Pepperdine University and lives in Studio City, CA with her supportive and sweet husband Andrew, two fabulous daughters, Emily & Charlotte and her German Shepherd-Kishu mix Watson the Wonder Dog. She has owned SarahBear's Cards & Creations since 2006, enjoys making cards and albums, listening to a cappella singing groups, swing dancing, cooking and raising money for her kids' school!

## **SPECIAL THANKS**

I could not have done this alone. There are many people who helped make this book a reality. As with everything in life, we stand on the shoulders of those who have come before us; those who have fundraised longer (or just have older kids)! Thank you to everyone who shared ideas and successes with me. Thanks for letting me know what worked (as well as what didn't). Each of the people listed below made an impact and helped me by sharing their thoughts on fundraising, family, and our future!

*My California Family*

Kirsten Abdo, Cindy Abrams, Lauren Albrecht, Rachel Bachmann, Brian Baker, Adina Barco, Andrew Barrett-Weiss, Dominique Barnet, Lisa Bates, Anthony & Rebecca Benenati, Lily Bettina Zaga, Janet Billig-Rich, Nickie Bryar Block, Jo Ann Burton, Myrna Cohen, Jane Cooper, Sheryl Craig Cooper, Beth D'Addario, Susan Dalrymple, Samantha Davis, Sarah Davis, Alice Ellis, Andrea Epinger, Tracey Feder, Pattie Fitzgerald, Andee Flynn, Nicki Genovese, Bill & Heidi Goverman, Oona Hanson, Mark & Donna Johnston, Arlene Kehela, Carley Knobloch, Anita Kuzmarskis, Yvette Lee, Jennifer Levinson, Lisa Libatique, Katie Lipsitt, Janet Loeb, Denise Luria, Cindy Malouf, Joe & Carmen Martinez, Cyndi Menegaz, Beth McCarthy-Miller, Nancy McIlvaney, Eric Miller, Toby & Cindy Northcote-Smith, Mary Odson, Kelly O'Shaughnessy, Ilyse Pallenberg, Kathy Paul, Danielle Peretz, Linda Perry, Mindi Pfeifer, Debbie Pisaro, Sharon Rotmensz, Marjan Sagheb, Amber Schaeffer, Maggie Scott, Bill and David Seymour, Robert Shadpour, Debi Sher, Andrew Silver, Bridget Smith, Maty Stern, Maggie Storm, Scott Svonkin, Mike Szymanski, Heather Tonkins, Paul Torres, Stavroula Tzanis Doukas, Joe Utsler, Nicole Walker, Bill Wright

## *My MMs*

Heather McCarron Allard, Melissa Bolton, Sarah Burns, Linsay Chavez, Amy Friend, Nikole (awesome cover design) Gipps, Karen Gunton, Jackie Hennessey, Karen Lee, Laura Magu, Prerna Malik, Rebecca Glaser Rabson, Lane Snifflin Rebelo, Ann Samoilov, Ellen Zimmerman

## *Parents from Around The USA*

Brandie Brasile-Stewart, Jamie Romanick Buss, Nika Corwin, Michele Maranian Curth,Katie Dawson, Bonnie Blander Dean, Louise Edington, Tara Gentile, Kristi Steele Griem, Katie Duval Haddock, Holly Reisem Hanna, Christin Harley, , Shannon Thomas Huckvale, Theresa Kilcourse, Natalie Kurlander, Mike Michalowicz, Fiona Morris, Naomi Naughton, Jennifer Penson, Tina Raksin

Made in the USA
Charleston, SC
15 May 2013